"I MUST BE INVOLVED IN THE STRUGGLE FOR JUSTICE

. . . whether it concerns a white man or a black man. If a black man's rights are being denied, I must be committed to his fight. . . . If a white man's rights are being denied, I must stand against my black brother in order to rectify that wrong. . . ."

"I am not interested in overthrowing white society any more than I am interested in allowing white society to overthrow black society. I am interested in overthrowing injustice. I am interested in dealing with inequality. I am interested in setting wrongs right. Because those are the principles of the Kingdom of God."

—Tom Skinner

How Black
Is the Gospel?

Tom Skinner

TRUMPET BOOKS
published by
A. J. HOLMAN COMPANY
division of J. B. LIPPINCOTT COMPANY
PHILADELPHIA and NEW YORK

Published by Pillar Books for A. J. Holman Company
Trumpet edition published August, 1976

Printed in the United States of America

ISBN: 0-87981-061-0

Contents

I Introduction

The struggle for social justice and human dignity in America has been erroneously identified as "the Negro problem." Many Americans view this crisis in simple terms of black and white. And since the value of the soul as well as the flesh is at stake, it is inevitable that religion be injected into the debate.

Many black Americans bitterly denounce Christianity and the Bible because, in their view, those who practice religious piety are among the leading exponents of hate, bigotry and prejudice. They feel that these "Bible-toting saints" perpetuate the most segregated hour of the week—eleven o'clock Sunday morning.

Today's young blacks, having learned more history than their forebears, are quick to resent acts of so-called Christianity and the use of those random Biblical verses that are so blatantly detrimental to the dignity of the black man in America.

There must have been thousands of slaves who vowed when they learned to read that they would never look at or allow their children to see those passages of St. Paul which encourage servants to be obedient to their masters. In many instances these were the only portions of the Bible that "ole massa" would allow the

preacher to read to illiterate black men, in the hope
that obedience to the Scriptures would further secure
the system of white supremacy.

This spirit still lives. America was born with a gro-
tesque, cancerous disease called slavery. The disease
lingers to this day in many forms and subtle variations.
The plantation mentality is still with us. Sometimes it
masquerades as democracy and free enterprise, but the
effect is the same on the spirits of the poor and dispos-
sessed.

When black men moved indoors to work in industry
and business, they found themselves imprisoned behind
ghetto walls of institutional racism. Nothing really had
changed. Those who headed the system went to church,
of course. They were seen as self-appointed Christians
worshiping in their white church, serving their best in-
terests in the name of their white god.

White Americans generally seem to think of black
people as inherently happy, basketball-bouncing children, dumb, lazy and basically content with their lot in
life—or at least they should be. Many whites are convinced that black people, commonly referred to as
"they," would never have become concerned about
their civil rights in the first place had not the Commu-
nists stirred them up. Black clergymen who become involved in the cause are considered by many whites to
be agitators who have left their calling to meddle in
matters clearly outside the will of God. "What those
people need is the gospel."

Black America is not about to follow a white Christ.
The image of a Christ patterned after Sallman's portrait
is more than suspect. It has become a contemptuous
symbol to the black man of all the fakery and chica-

nery endorsed by so many white Christians. If Christ takes on the image of an Anglo-Saxon Protestant suburbanite, He's obviously not for black men. It is inconceivable that this kind of Christ would die for black people.

The question is, of course, whether this view of Jesus Christ is true. Has Christianity become the "worship of white," used as a tool of oppression to increase the black man's burden? If this be true, it is understandable that the black man must find his salvation through worshiping black.

One thing is certain: whatever contemporary man decides about the "color" of religion, Christ stands outside that debate. Even a superficial reading of the gospel reveals that Christ showed only one special interest—allegiance to His Father and the Kingdom of God. He was owned by no man, He belonged to no particular group, and He refused to sanction one party or system over another. He was God in the form of man—neither black nor white.

No specific mention of color, other than the reference to Moses' marrying a black woman, appears in the Scriptures. Racism as we know it today was not an issue in Biblical times.

A question still persists: "All right, granted that Jesus Christ was neither black nor white, Protestant nor Catholic, and did not embrace Christianity as a system. But if Christ was essentially concerned with the spiritual condition of man, how can He relate to the issues of today? How can He respond to the political, economic and social needs of the black American?"

Christ offered Himself to Israel but was rejected because He refused to accommodate His spiritual revolution to Jewish political ambitions. His kingdom is not of this world, which explains His rejection of militarism.

Christ taught His followers to be just in their dealings with men and to love each other. Leadership was redefined in terms of service, and labor was elevated from an exercise in self-interest to a means of helping those in need. Family relations were hallowed and sex given a Godly status. This transforms the issue of politics and economics from a reluctant response to law to a wholesome affirmation of love for one's fellow man. Brotherly love, as it is commonly known, is extended to embrace all men.

Once again the question is asked, Can the crisis in human relations be solved through a Christianity that has become identified as the white man's religion? No, not as long as it reflects faith in scientism, secularism and racism. What success, then, would result from establishing a black religion? Scarcely more, since the tendency here is to make a god of blackness; and surely black is no less self-centered than white.

In the Bible the call is: "Turn to me and be saved, all the ends of the earth! For I am God, and there is no other."[1] The issue is not "religion," whatever its name, whatever its origin, for "religion" is a set of values that best suits an individual's life, and the white man's set of values cannot possibly solve the problems of the black man. In fact, these values are the very ones that keep these problems from being solved.

Christ did not come to save society but to redeem individuals from the curse of sin. But He still made it

[1]Isaiah 45:22. (All quotations from the Bible follow the Revised Standard Version unless otherwise noted.)

clear that the application of truth is not just an individual matter. He declared that in the end nations would be judged largely on the basis of their treatment of those who were less privileged.

If the problems of society are to be solved, this will only occur when men take their fate out of the hands of other men and place it in the hands of Christ. "Blessed is the nation whose God is the Lord."[2]

In the midst of America's racial crisis, Christianity in its pure and true form alone can make the difference. The black man, who has made noteworthy contributions to American life and culture in spite of oppression, is in an ideal position to lead a spiritual crusade. The white man needs to swallow his pride and seek forgiveness for racist attitudes that have brought on the present crisis in America. The black man, then, must forgive in a true demonstration of Christian love.

If the white man will take the initiative, he will find a cooperative response. Neither action will be more than skin deep unless Christ Himself is in control.

If you want to change a man truly, you must change him from the inside out. You can't really change him by just altering his environment. The problems of man are basically theological in nature; their ultimate solutions will only be realized if man accepts the peace terms laid down by God.

It has been said that you can't pass a law to make one man love another. However, most of the ills of our society do not call for love but for justice. It is at the point where a man needs justice that laws must be passed.

Laws must be passed to create a climate for justice

[2]Psalms 33:12.

Laws do not create a climate for love; they are not intended to do that. From a scriptural point of view it is love which transcends law and not law which transcends love. The truly Bible-oriented man seeks always to balance love and justice.

The answer to bigotry, hate and prejudice rests in a transformation of the individual through Jesus Christ. But there is a difference between personal and institutional prejudice; while the Christian is called upon to recognize the difference, he is equally responsible to address his message to both. Here he finds himself in the prophetic line of Micah, Isaiah and Jeremiah.

Man as an individual must find peace with God before he will be able to live at peace with his fellow man.

The final solution is in His hands, and His hands are neither white nor black.

II The Black Past

Any understanding of the black revolution, any understanding of the black man's rage, must come from a knowledge of his violent past. To understand the gospel of Jesus Christ and its implications for the black revolution, we must examine the black man's history. We must go back over the years to 1619, when a ship with no name, with a captain by the name of Jope and an English pilot by the name of Marmaduke, landed in Jamestown, Virginia. That ship began the history of the black man in America—one year before the *Mayflower*. There were approximately twenty black people aboard, and notable among them was a couple known as Isabella and Antony.

These early black settlers were not slaves. In fact, between 1619 and 1660 there was no slave system in the colonies, nor was there any racial inferiority. Our country had what were known as "indentured servants." This system enabled poor white immigrants to sell their services in America for a stipulated number of years. Under this system religious dissenters, ex-convicts, and prostitutes, among others, were brought to the colonies and sold to the highest bidder. These people then worked off the amount paid for them and finally were set free. There were black indentured servants and white indentured servants. Black people held such servants as well as white people.

During this time, blacks owned land, voted, and testified in court; they held positions of authority; they lived side by side with whites in social and economic equality; they made love to each other and bore children by each other. Kenneth M. Stampp puts it this way: "Negro and white servants of the seventeenth century seemed to be remarkably unconcerned about their visible physical differences. They toiled together in the fields, fraternized during leisure hours, and, in and out of wedlock, collaborated in siring a numerous progeny."[1]

By 1660, with the growth of cotton and tobacco plantations, a larger labor force was needed. The system of indentured servitude could have been continued, but it was expensive. There was the possibility of enslaving the Indians and keeping a free labor system for both blacks and whites. But Indians made poor slaves: they were weak and often sickly and, knowing the countryside so well, found it easy to run away.

All indentured servants might have been enslaved, but this posed problems too. When a white escaped, it was very difficult to recapture him because he could easily blend with the rest of society. Also, white servants tended to be "Christianized." It was very difficult for one Christian to justify enslaving another. Most important, white men were usually the subjects of strong European governments, to which they could appeal for protection.

Black people did not have any of these "disadvan-

[1]Stampp, *The Peculiar Institution*, pp. 21–22.

tages." They were strong, healthy, visible, cheap, numerous—and unprotected. Thus in Virginia and Maryland in the 1660's, laws were passed making Negroes servants for life. Intermarriage was prohibited, and children of Negro women became bond or free, depending on their mother's condition.

At first, religion was used as an excuse: it was thought to be all right to enslave a non-Christian. Soon even Christianized blacks were made available; in 1667, a Virginia law stated that "the conferring of baptisme does not alter the condition of the person as to his bondage or freedom."[2] Color became the mark of bondage. It was simple from that point on to develop the slave system and to maintain it.

This is one reason that the black community today considers Christianity the white man's religion, given to the black man only in order to keep him in his place. Christianity was used in the Western Hemisphere for many hundreds of years to maintain the white man's economic, political and social control over the black man.

Sixty years after Isabella and Antony landed on American soil, sixty years after black people helped found this country, the European slave trade had reached its height. It is said that Africa lost more than forty million people, half of whom reached the New World. Lerone Bennett, Jr., in his book *Before the Mayflower,* puts it this way:

These figures, though instructive, do not say anything meaningful about the people involved.

[2]Quoted in Lerone Bennett, Jr., *Before the Mayflower,* pp. 37–38.

The slave trade was not a statistic, however astronomical. The slave trade was people living, lying, stealing, murdering and dying. The slave trade was a black man who stepped out of his hut for a breath of fresh air and ended up, ten months later, in Georgia with bruises on his back and a brand on his chest.

The slave trade was a black mother suffocating her newborn baby because she didn't want him to grow up a slave.

The slave trade was a kind captain forcing his suicide-minded passengers to eat by breaking their teeth, though, as he said, he was "naturally compassionate."

The slave trade was a bishop sitting on an ivory chair on a wharf in the Congo and extending his fat hand in wholesale baptism of slaves who were rowed beneath him, going in chains to the slave ships.

The slave trade was a greedy king raiding his own villages to get slaves to buy brandy.

The slave trade was a pious captain holding prayer services twice a day on his slave ship and writing later the famous hymn, "How Sweet the Name of Jesus Sounds."

The slave trade was deserted villages, bleached bones on slave trails and people with no last names.[3]

The slave trade was so prosperous that, by 1710, the number of blacks in the colonies had increased to fifty thousand. By 1776, there were five hundred thousand.

[3]Bennett, *op. cit.*, pp. 30–31.

By 1860, there were four million black people in America.

They came from Africa's West Coast. Some were kidnapped; some were sold by their own tribes for breaking native laws or were captured inland in native wars. They were forced to march hundreds of miles over mountains and rivers to the coast, where they were inspected and then packed into slave ships, barefoot and naked, chained ankle to ankle. Not all these slaves were poor Africans. Some were priests, princes, warriors, merchants, nobles. At least once, for instance, an African sold another African one day and was captured himself and sold the next.

These Africans were packed into the holds of ships between decks which sometimes were no farther apart than eighteen inches. It was impossible to turn or shift with ease. For however long the voyage took, the slaves were forced to live like animals. If an epidemic or sickness swept the ship, the trip was unendurable. Imagine, if you will, being chained neck to neck and ankle to ankle, not being able to turn around; sometimes chained to the deck by your neck and legs. Many slaves went mad "before dying or suffocating. In their frenzy some killed others in the hope of procuring more room to breathe. Men strangled those next to them, and women drove nails into each other's brains." This contemporary report goes on to say that it was not unusual to find a dead man chained to a living one. "So many dead people were thrown overboard on slavers that it was said that sharks would pick up a ship off the coast of Africa and follow it to America."[4]

Whenever new slaves were purchased for a planta-

[4]*Ibid.*, p. 41.

tion, they were broken up into groups where certain "trusted" slaves initiated them into the ways of slave life. These "drivers" were allowed to withhold food and punish the newcomers in other ways. They taught them how to speak the language and do the work. After one year, when it was assumed that a slave had been broken in and tamed, the master or overseer of the plantation took over.

The irony of this whole situation is that, during slavery, Americans were making tremendous poetic statements about liberty and justice and freedom. As Lerone Bennett points out:

> There lived in Connecticut in the days preceding the Revolution a patriotic preacher who was given to making pretty speeches about liberty or death. This preacher owned a slave named Jack. The preacher preached and Jack slaved and listened and wondered. One day Jack went to his master and said:
>
> "Master, I observe you always keep preaching about liberty and praying for liberty, and I love to hear you, sir, for liberty be a good thing. You preach well and you pray well; but one thing you remember, Master—poor Jack ain't free yet."[5]

The irony intensified as the colonies, with half a million slaves, decided to fight for the belief that all men were created equal and entitled to "life, liberty and the pursuit of happiness."

The first man to die in the American Revolution in Boston was Crispus Attucks, a black man. Black men,

[5]*Ibid.*, pp. 48–49.

some of them slaves, went out and fought on the front lines and virtually signed the Declaration of Independence with their lives. Black men lived, bled and died so that white men could be free.

Some men who preached liberty and justice recognized the black man's commitment—such as Thomas Jefferson, who was also a slaveholder. When he wrote the Declaration of Independence, he inserted a clause which accused the King of England of promoting slavery. The clause read: "He has waged cruel war against human nature itself, violating its most sacred rights of life and liberty in the person of a distant people who never offended him, captivating and carrying them into slavery in another hemisphere, or to incur miserable death in their transportation."[6]

It is very interesting that this clause was struck out in order to keep slaveholders and traders happy. Many of them had serious questions about that sentence, "All men are created equal." Who were "all men"? At this point the rationalization developed that the black man was not in fact a man. Perhaps one could accept the notion that all *men* were created equal if the black man was not really a man! The supposition was thus introduced that the black was subhuman, an animal, subjected to the white man's whims by "the decree of God." As thousands and thousands of blacks died on their way to the New World, as thousands were thrown overboard, as thousands suffered and were killed on the plantations, there arose the inevitable question from whites with moral and ethical consciences: "How do you justify the killing of so many people?" How conve-

[6]Cited in Bennett, *op. cit.*, pp. 49–52.

nient to answer, "But they are not people; they are subhuman!"

Slavery was upheld by three sectors of society: religious, economic, and political. First was the church. Slavery was seen as a divine institution, ordained by God. White pastors throughout the country preached that God had ordained the black man to his condition of servitude. The most quoted story was the incident in the book of Genesis where Noah goes to bed drunk one night. His drunkenness and nakedness is mocked by his son, Canaan. The following morning when Noah discovers what Canaan has done, he curses Canaan. It was argued that Canaan, being a descendant of Ham (Ham meaning Black) was black, and therefore God had cursed all black people and relegated them to a condition of servitude.

Slaves were allowed to have "praying parties," held on Sundays. But what the master allowed to be taught was the virtue of dutiful obedience. One overseer was told that there would be no objection to the slaves hearing the Gospel "in its original purity and simplicity," which meant Ephesians, chapter 6, verse 5: "Servants, be obedient to them that are your masters" (King James Version).[7]

Fortunately, though, not many slaves were deceived by these readings. The God who delivered the Israelites was more meaningful to them. You could hear this coming out of the slave quarters in such songs as "Didn't my Lord deliver Daniel? Then why not every man?" Slaves would slip away into the fields to pour out their troubles to God. There are indications that fantastic spiritual awakenings and revivals took place.

[7]*Ibid.*, p. 80.

"I went down in the valley to pray; my soul got happy and I stayed all day."

Most songs rose from the sorrow and pain of slavery.

> I know moon-rise, I know star-rise,
>   Lay dis body down.
> I walk in de moonlight, I walk in de starlight,
>   To lay dis body down.
> I'll walk in de graveyard, I'll walk through de graveyard
>   To lay dis body down.
> I'll lie in de grave and stretch out my arms;
>   Lay dis body down.
> I go to de judgement in de evenin' of de day,
>   When I lay dis body down;
> And my soul and your soul will meet in de day
>   When I lay dis body down.

Hearing this song during the Civil War, Thomas Wentworth Higginson wrote, "Never, it seems to me, since man first lived and suffered, was his infinite longing for peace uttered more plaintively than in that line [the refrain]."[8]

Out of the religious meetings in the slave camps developed what was known as the "ring shout." According to anthropologist Ernest Borneman, it was "a straight adaptation of African ceremonialism to Christian liturgy." Much of this practice survives today in some "shouting" churches in the black community. The

[8]Higginson, *Army Life in a Black Regiment* (Boston, 1870), p. 209.

"ring shout" was described in the *Nation* magazine as follows:

> The benches are pushed back to the wall, when the formal meeting is over, and old and young, men and women, sprucely-dressed young men, grotesquely half-clad field hands—the women generally with gay handkerchiefs twisted about their heads and with short skirts, boys with tattered shirts and men's trousers, young girls barefooted—all stand up in the middle of the floor, and when the "sperichil" is struck up, begin first walking, and by-and-by shuffling round, one after the other, in a ring. The foot is hardly taken from the floor, and the progression is mainly due to a jerking, hitching motion which agitates the entire shouter, and soon brings out streams of perspiration. Sometimes he dances silently, sometimes as he shuffles he sings the chorus of the spiritual, and sometimes the song itself is also sung by the dancers. But more frequently a band, composed of some of the best singers and of tired shouters, stand at the side of the room to "base" the others, singing the body of the song and clapping their hands together or on the knees. Songs and dance are alike extremely energetic, and often, when the shout lasts into the middle of the night, the monotonous thud, thud of the feet prevents sleep within half a mile of the praise-shout.[9]

The second sector of society that upheld slavery was the economic sector. Slavery was a cheap form of labor

[9] Quoted in Bennett, *op. cit.*, pp. 81–82.

that made it possible for the slaveowner to compete with foreign cotton markets. Healthy male slaves in those days sold for $600; healthy females for $300. And the slave master, having purchased a healthy male and a healthy female, could go on to build himself a valuable work force.

The third sector that upheld slavery was the political system. Laws were passed throughout the South regulating both the behavior and the trading of slaves. (Politics and economics in our country run hand in hand; and generally whoever controls the economy of a nation, whoever has the most influence in the economic sector of any community, tends to wield that same influence in the political structure.)

In some cases families were allowed to exist on the slave plantations. Marriages between slaves were not recognized by the state, but many slave masters allowed people to get "married" by permitting them to live together. When a ceremony was performed, either by the overseer or an itinerant preacher, no marriage certificate was given. The words that put them together could be "until death or *distance* do you part"[10]—the couple could be separated tomorrow on the slave blocks.

Many slave plantations kept what was known as a "stud," a healthy male slave whose sole job was to impregnate healthy female slaves in order to breed healthy children. When the woman became pregnant, the man was moved to another quarter. Within a course of ten years, he could have sired a hundred children, but he was never allowed to be a father to any of them. Nor were most slave women allowed to raise

[10]Quoted in Stampp, *op. cit.*, p. 344.

their children past the milking stage. While the mothers worked in the fields, their children stayed in a nursery together.

A great deal of romantic nonsense has been written to perpetuate the myth of the "docile" Negro slave. The planter of the day knew better, from bitter experience. Black men, oppressed, were dangerous. The Negro might bow and scrape, but he also poisoned food, cut throats, set fire to plantations, ran away, and plotted massacres. Events in Haiti in 1791, where slaves rose up and slaughtered their white masters, terrified slaveowners everywhere. Some white men and women, weakened under the strain of living in constant fear, went mad or died of heart failure.

Charles S. Johnson writes about black docility:

> Denmark Vesey, a Negro who resisted slavery and led an insurrection in the effort to throw off the oppression, is a type which contradicts the assumption that Negroes are innately docile as a race and were content with slavery. In a sense, Vesey represents the spirit of Independence for which the founding fathers of America are praised —an insurrection is merely an unsuccessful revolution. But Denmark Vesey is a symbol of a spirit too violent to be acceptable to the white community. There are no Negro schools named for him, and it would be extremely poor taste and bad judgement for the Negroes to take any pride in his courage and philosophy. There is, indeed, little chance for Negro youth to know about him at all.[11]

[11]Quoted in Bennett, *op. cit.*, p .96.

The desire of the black man to be free expressed itself not only in revolt but in more passive forms of resistance. Not only were crops set on fire, cattle "accidentally" stampeded, slaveowners poisoned, there were countless slowdowns, desertions, and deliberate acts of stupidity. Everything the black man did in his relationship with the slave planter and in his relationship with fellow slaves was in keeping with the fact that he wanted to be free.

After much rhetoric, revolt and rebellion came 1865 and the Emancipation Proclamation. The black man was set free. But all Emancipation did was to decide what the black man was not; it never defined what he was. Emancipation merely said, The black man is not a slave; it never defined him as a man.

To this former slave, society said, "Now that you are free, you are to settle down, become the husband of one wife, be the father of your own children, and acculturated into American life"—in other words, you are to unlearn in one night what you have been taught for 250 years. The amazing thing was that he began to do it. Through programs of self-help and self-determination, the black man sought to pull himself up by the bootstraps—but it wasn't easy.

Immediately after the Civil War, many provisional Southern governments set up by President Johnson enacted what were known as "Black Codes," as a way of re-establishing slavery. By means of so-called "vagrancy laws," these codes generally kept black people from moving. The South Carolina legislature forbade black people to work in any capacity except farming and menial service without a special license.

> The legislature also gave "masters" the right to whip "servants" under eighteen years of age. In other states, Negroes could be punished for "insulting gestures," "seditious speeches," and the "crime" of walking off a job. Negroes could not preach in one state without police permission. A Mississippi law enacted in November [1865] required Negroes to have jobs before the second Monday in January.[12]

Whites who were angry because the South lost the war worked off their pent-up emotions on unarmed blacks. Some former slave masters forcefully kept their former slaves on their plantations. Other white men patroled the country roads in armed bands; the dead bodies of murdered blacks could be found by the roadsides. According to Lerone Bennett, "Hundreds of freedmen were massacred in 'riots' staged and directed by policemen and other government officials"; in Memphis, Tennessee, for example, in May, 1866, forty-six black people were killed and seventy-five were wounded, five black women were raped by white men, and twelve schools and four churches were burned.[13]

General Carl Schurz put it this way in a special investigation he made for President (Andrew) Johnson:

[12]Bennett, *op. cit.*, p. 192.
[13]*Ibid.*, p. 193

The emancipation of the slave is submitted to only in so far as chattel slavery in the old form could not be kept up. But although the freedman is no longer considered the property of the individual master, he is considered the slave of society. . . . Wherever I go—the street, the shop, the house, the hotel, or the steamboat—I hear the people talk in such a way as to indicate that they are yet unable to conceive of the Negro as possessing any rights at all. Men who are honorable in their dealings with their white neighbors will cheat a Negro without feeling a single twinge of their honor. To kill a Negro, they do not deem murder; to debauch a Negro woman, they do not think fornication; to take the property away from a Negro, they do not consider robbery. The people boast that when they get freedmen's affairs in their own hands, to use their own expression, "the niggers will catch hell."[14]

In spite of these overwhelming odds, black people rose to political power between 1865 and 1875. In South Carolina, the first reconstruction legislature had 84 blacks and 73 whites. In the thirty years that followed the Emancipation, South Carolina sent eight black congressmen to the House. In the state of Mississippi, the first state legislature had 40 blacks and 75 whites. Mississippi sent two black men to the United States Senate and one to the House. Louisiana's first reconstruction legislature had 49 blacks and 88 whites. Three of Louisiana's lieutenant governors and one congressman were black, and one black was elected to

[14]Quoted in *ibid.*, pp. 193–194.

the United States Senate. The first reconstruction legislature in Florida had 19 blacks and 57 whites. The secretary of state was black, the superintendent of education was black, and so was one congressman. In the state of North Carolina, the first legislature had 19 blacks and 135 whites; four congressmen during reconstruction went to Washington from North Carolina. Alabama had 26 blacks and 58 whites in the state legislature and three black congressmen. Georgia had 32 blacks and 213 whites in their legislature and one black congressman. Virginia had 27 blacks and 154 whites and one black congressman.

But as black people moved into power, whites could not tolerate it. The beginning of the end of the black man in public political life in America during Reconstruction took place in 1877 in the Presidential race between Republican Rutherford B. Hayes and Democrat Samuel J. Tilden. Election results were being disputed in South Carolina, Louisiana and Florida, where black people had substantial voting power. The election ended up in the House of Representatives, and a group of Southern Democrats launched a filibuster which prevented an orderly count of the electoral votes. A compromise had to be reached. Mr. Hayes, to win the Presidency, entered into a signed agreement with Southern politicians that, if elected, he would withdraw troops from the South, end reconstruction and allow white people in the South to deal with black people in their own way. Lerone Bennett comments:

The bargain was arranged in a series of conferences which reached a climax, ironically enough, in a fashionable hotel owned by James Wormley, a well-to-do Negro businessman. . . .

The bargain was signed, sealed and delivered. The Southerners called off the filibuster, Hayes was elected, the troops were withdrawn, and the South began the long process of whipping the Negroes into submission.[15]

Jim Crow laws were passed to separate blacks and whites during their lives in public conveyances, hospitals, orphanages, prisons and asylums and after death in funeral homes, morgues and cemeteries. In Mobile, Alabama, black people had to be off the streets by 10 p.m. In Birmingham, blacks and whites were prevented by law from playing checkers together. Black people were denied the right to vote, through poll taxes, literacy tests, and white primaries.

The story is told of a Negro teacher, a graduate of Harvard, who presented himself to a Mississippi registrar. The teacher read the state constitution and several books. The registrar came up with a passage in Latin, which the teacher read, and a passage in Greek, which the teacher read, and pages in French, German and Spanish, all of which the teacher read. Finally the registrar held up a page of Chinese characters and asked, "What does this mean?" The teacher replied: "It means you don't want me to vote."[16]

By such unjust and absurd literacy tests, the black

[15]Bennett, *op. cit.*, p. 218.
[16]*Ibid.*, p. 234.

man was excluded from the electorate. Ben Tillman, the South Carolina demagogue, put it this way: "We have done our level best; we have scratched our heads to find out how we could eliminate the last one of them. We stuffed ballot boxes. We shot them. We are not ashamed of it."[17] W. K. Vardaman told a cheering crowd, "The way to control the nigger is to whip him when he does not obey without it, and another is never to pay him more wages than is actually necessary to buy food and clothing."[18]

Between 1877 and 1925, thousands of black people were lynched, their women raped, their children beaten and their homes burned; they were disenfranchised and relegated to fourth-class citizenship, and during that period of time virtually no white person was arrested, tried, or convicted for a crime against a black man.

When World War I came, the black man put on the American Army uniform and went off to defend America, "the land of the free and the home of the brave," and those democratic principles that had so notably been denied him.

Partly as a result of blacks being stationed in the armed forces in many of the large cities in the North, such cities as New York, Chicago, San Francisco, Los Angeles, word began to trickle back to the South, where 90 percent of the black population then lived, that if black people went North they would find greater economic, social and political opportunities. Between 1920 and 1950 there was a mass movement of blacks to Northern cities.

[17]Ibid., p. 235.
[18]Ibid.

When he arrived in the North, the black man discovered that the patterns of segregation were not too different. He could rent or buy a house only in certain neighborhoods, and he soon discovered that whenever black people moved into a community, large numbers of whites moved out, so that integration began to be defined as that period between the time that the first black family moves into a community and the last white family moves out. He soon discovered that, where Negro neighborhoods developed, the city no longer provided the same kind of services. Schools and hospitals became run-down. Building-code inspectors no longer enforced the laws; sanitation departments no longer collected the garbage as frequently,

These conditions created a climate in which the black man's struggle knew no geographical limitation. Now—both in the North and in the South—he had to fight for equality in education, jobs and housing and, above all, for his own human dignity, in his own eyes and in the eyes of his white brother—to discover who he was and to take his rightful place in society.

The greatest tragedy in all of the black man's history in this country has been the strange silence of the white church in America. This is not to say that there have been no voices raised in protest. But they have been few and feeble. For the most part, the white church in America has maintained the status quo and upheld the social system. How different from the radical, revolutionary gospel of Bible times, when believers addressed themselves to the roots of injustice and sinful egotism!

The issue that is now before us is: How can an institution which itself has been infested with racism, which has denied black people equality, which has preached a message of separation and segregation, which has sought to use itself to prove that black people were socially, economically and spiritually inferior—how can that church now take a message which it was supposed to have been preaching for all these years and make it relevant to the black community?

Our argument in this book is that true Christianity has never really been applied to the sphere of black-white relations in this country. We therefore set ourselves the task of showing how true Christianity—the real message of Christ—can speak with decisiveness and truth to today's black revolution.

III   The Meaning of the Gospel

If we are to consider the question of how black the gospel is—and by that we mean how relevant is the message of Jesus Christ to the black man's condition, how relevant is the gospel to the black man's struggle, how relevant is the gospel to the black revolution?—we must consider what the nature of the gospel is. What is this thing called the gospel?

This is a question that sometimes goes unanswered, not only in black circles but in white circles as well. While many black people credit the white man with being the originator of Christianity in the Western world, the black man has failed to understand that the white man himself may not really know the essence of the gospel.

But there are those who do know what the essence of the gospel is and have refused to make it applicable to the black situation in America. They have refused to apply it to their own lives in terms of their relationships with their black brother.

It seems to me that there are four main crises faced by the black man in his revolutionary struggle, four crises that the gospel of Jesus Christ must deal with. If the gospel is to have any validity at all, it will be in its ability to deal with these crises.

The first is the crisis of the black man's past: whether he can overcome the years of slavery, the years of mental, political, economic and social enslavement, the years of subjection to fourth-class citizenship and disenfranchisement, and the rage that is within him as a result of his past.

Second is the crisis of the black man's identity: his struggle to discover himself, who he is, what he is here for and where he is going.

Third is the crisis of community, both the black man's relationship with his black brother and also his relationship with his white brother: whether or not the black community can survive and, more, provide leadership in American society.

And fourth is the crisis of power: having discovered his past and learned how to overcome it, having discovered who he is and who his neighbor is and how he ought to relate to him, the black man must find the power to pull it off. At this point he faces the same problem his white brother faces. The white brother has had no problem in discovering his past and overcoming it, he has had no problem discovering who he is, he knows what his responsibility ought to be toward his neighbor—but he has never had the power to pull it off.

To understand what has brought on these crises—the crisis of his past, the crisis of who he is, the crisis of community and the crisis of power—we must go back to the very beginning; we must go back to where it all started, because it is here that we will discover the essence of the gospel. I mean those emphatic statements in the Bible in the early chapters of Genesis. In Genesis 1:26, God said, "Let us make man in our image, after our likeness." And Genesis 2:7 says that "then the Lord God formed man of dust from the ground and breathed into his nostrils the breath of life; and man became a living being."

The "image" of God does not mean that man looked like God or that man was a perfect replica of God; the Bible says that God breathed the breath of life and man became a living being. It was the purpose of the invisible God to mirror Himself in man. It was the purpose of God to take the common clay of man's humanity, breathe His own life through that man and put that man on open display in a world He had created for him as a living testimony that the invisible God could come alive through the humanity of a man. And that is still God's purpose—it has not changed. It is the purpose of God to take you exactly the way you are, and as you are willing to make yourself available to Him; it is the will of God to live His life through you, with your two feet planted on the earth.

The Bible says that God left this man some very simple instructions. God told him to have dominion over the beasts of the field, the birds of the air, and over everything that crawls upon the face of the earth. It was God's intention that man be a superintendent in charge of God's universe. It was the will of God that man's life be thrilling and adventurous. He said to man, "You may freely eat of every tree in the garden."[1] Trees represent life. In essence, God was saying, I want you to enjoy life; I want you to live life to its hilt; I want you to have a ball.

[1]Genesis 2:16.

There are a number of people who are under the strange illusion that to be a Christian means that God wants to box you in, that God wants to impose a lot of rules and regulations and restrictions. But here God is saying to the first man, to whom He has given this beautiful paradise, I want you to enjoy life; I want life to be thrilling and adventurous for you.

God said, "You may freely eat of every tree in the garden; but of the tree of the knowledge of good and evil you shall not eat, for in the day that you eat of it you shall die."[2]

Now there were two trees in that garden, representing two basic ways of life. One was the tree of life, which represented God Himself. And God was in essence saying, If you eat of Me (the word "eat" means to depend upon), if you allow Me to be the captain of your soul, the master of your fate, if you depend completely upon Me to be your life, to be the fountain from which all of your life flows, if you allow Me to be the pivot of your existence, the ground of your being, you will live. Life will be exciting and thrilling and adventurous because I, God, Who am life, will be life in you. And so the tree of life represented dependency upon the life of the Creator.

But in that garden there was another tree, and it was called the tree of the knowledge of good and evil. It represented the very antithesis of the tree of life; it represented independence from God. If man had eaten of that tree, he would have been clenching his fist in the face of God and telling God to get off his back. He would have been saying, in essence, I appreciate the fact, God, that You have made me; I appreciate the

[2]*Ibid.*, 16-17.

fact that You put me in this beautiful paradise; I appreciate the fact that I have mental faculties with which to make a choice. And I choose, from here on in, to run the show; I choose to be my own god. I will be the captain of my own fate, the master of my own soul, the origin of my own image and the ground of my own being.

So that was man's choice: whether he would live his life in total dependency upon the God who made him, living and deriving his life from the life of his Creator Who is life, or whether he would be independent, detaching himself from the life of his creator and becoming his own god. This is the choice all humanity faces.

In the third chapter of Genesis, the Bible says that that personality, that force of evil, that spirit of evil in the universe called Satan, who has set himself in diametric opposition to the plan, will and program of God, entered the garden and talked to the first woman about that tree. "Did God say, 'You shall not eat of any tree of the garden'?"[3] Now, God never said that. God has already emphatically said to man, "You may freely eat of every tree in the garden." I want you to enjoy life; there are no restrictions; you are not bound up by any rules and regulations. All I ask, if you are going to enjoy life and have access to all that I have made for you, is that you simply do it in Me—that you allow Me to be the basis from which you act.

It has always been a trick of Satan, down through the years, to give people the impression that it is the will of God that people be hemmed in. This is why they ask such questions of Christians as: "What do you do for pleasure? I suppose you just sit around and read the

[3] Genesis 3:1.

Bible and pray all day." The implication is that to be a Christian means to follow a set of restrictions. But this is not the case.

So Eve said, "We may eat of the fruit of the trees of the garden; but God said, 'You shall not eat of the fruit of the tree which is in the midst of the garden (that is, the tree of the knowledge of good and evil), neither shall you touch it, lest you die.'" Now, God never said "lest you die." God said, The day you decide to be independent, the day you decide to be your own god, the day you decide to be the captain of your own soul and the master of your own fate, that is the day "you shall die." Notice that the word "lest" means maybe not or maybe so; maybe God can't be trusted, maybe what God says isn't true. The reason why the world is in the rut that it is in, with men set against men, black against white, Democrat against Republican, tribe against tribe and culture against culture and religion against religion, is that the devil has always planted in man's mind the question as to whether or not God can be trusted; whether or not you can stake your life on what God says; whether or not God has integrity.

The Bible has emphatically stated, "The soul that sins shall die."[5] It is not, again, that God is some super-cop, ready to bust you as soon as you offend him. It is not that God deliberately takes a person and condemns him to hell simply because he doesn't do what He says. What God is saying is this: I am the life. I represent life. If you want to live, you've got to stay plugged into Me. If you detach yourself from Me, if

[4]*Ibid.*, 2–3.
[5]Ezekiel 18:20.

you act independently of me, you are dead, you don't
function.

Like a refrigerator: If you want that refrigerator to
work you'd better keep it plugged in. The electrical
juice comes out of that socket. Take the plug out of the
socket, and the refrigerator doesn't function because it
is not receiving any juice. God is saying, Man, I am the
power plant. I am the juice box. I am the fountain of
life. If you want to live, stay plugged into Me. Detach
yourself from Me, act independently of Me, pull yourself out of the socket, and you've had it! You cease to
live! You die!

Satan merely takes one word, a lie, and adds it to the
truth. He says in verses 4 and 5 of Genesis 3, "You
will not die. For God knows that when you eat of it
your eyes will be opened, and you will be like God,
knowing good and evil." In other words, he is telling
Eve, You will not die. God is not telling the truth; God
is trying to keep you boxed in. God knows that as soon
as you exercise some initiative, as soon as you become
independent, your eyes will be opened and you will be
as wise as He is, deciphering good and evil, able to
think for yourself. God is afraid of the competition.
That is why He wants you to live a restricted life, totally dependent upon Him, so He can drag you along
like a puppet.

Now you know, Eve, every time I've come to you
and asked you about something, you have given me
this line, "Let me find out what the Lord says." And
every time I have asked you a question, you've had to
go and find out what God says. Has God got you so
hoodwinked that you can't add two and two and get
four by yourself without running to God? Now, Eve, if

you listen to me, I will liberate you. I will make it possible for you to stand on your own two feet and be your own god. I will make it possible for you not to have to run to God for everything. You will be independent.

The Bible says that Eve looked at that idea. Here was an opportunity to be wise. And Eve and her husband, the first man, did depend upon their own intelligence and seek to derive their life from their own souls. And thus they sinned,

The Bible doesn't say that they committed any grossly immoral act—they didn't go out and shoot anybody, they didn't trip out, they didn't take any drugs, they didn't steal. They didn't do anything that society or the church would frown upon. They simply decided to be their own gods. They decided to stand on their own two feet and run their own lives. And that, my friend, is what sin is: independence from God.

It is unfortunate that too many people have tried to put sin into categories. This has been especially true of those who preach to black people. When you mention sin to the average black person, the first thing that comes to his mind is sexual immorality—the cat who is running around with another man's wife; the gal who is bearing an illegitimate child—or the guy who is drunk on the street, or the thief who is a drug addict. If you are not committing adultery, if you are not pregnant out of wedlock, if you are not taking drugs or stealing someone else's money, then in his mind you are a good Christian. That is not so.

The Scripture teaches that any person who is living his life independently of the life of God, no matter how moral he may be in his community, is a sinner because he is detached from the source of life; he is not plugged into God.

Now when man sinned, when man became independent, when he decided to be the captain of his own soul and the master of his own fate, the Bible declares that death occurred.

Sin did three things to that man. First, it separated him from God. The Bible says that God drove man out of the garden and away from His presence. Man lost one of his most priceless possessions—he lost fellowship with the living God. When a man decides to become independent, when he decides to unplug himself from the source of life, when he disconnects himself from the power, he dies. Just as the refrigerator ceases to function when unplugged, or the automobile won't go without its battery, or the power plant can't run without its generator, so man can't function without his God. When man became detached from the life of God, he lost fellowship with God and became uprooted. The source of his power was gone.

That is the issue with man today. If you ask the average person, "Look, friend, do you know God?" he will never really and directly answer your question.

He will say, "Well, I go to church every Sunday."

"No, that is not my question. Do you know God?"

He will say, "Well, I sing in the choir."

"No, that is not the issue. Do you know God?"

He will say, "Well, I take communion. I go to confession."

It is quite possible to be "religious"—to go to church, to sing in the choir, to be altar boy and take confession or communion—and not be plugged into the source of life.

The second thing sin did was to separate man from himself. When man gets unplugged from God, he also becomes disoriented. It takes God to be a man; God made man and breathed into him the breath of life. It takes God to be a man; without God in a man, he ceases to be man as God intended him to be. When man decided to be independent, to direct his own life and be the captain of his own soul, he was in essence saying, At this moment I renounce all right to function as a complete man. As a result he became uprooted. He no longer understood himself—why he was here, where he came from and where he was going. That is why man today—black, white, yellow, red or any other kind on the face of the earth—suffers from an identity crisis. A man who is not plugged into God cannot know who he is. He cannot function. He cannot do his thing.

The third thing that sin did was to separate man from his brother. Not too long after man sinned, Cain rose up and slew his brother, Abel, and then had the audacity to turn around and ask God, "Am I my brother's keeper?"[6] A man who does not know how to walk with God, a man who has detached himself from the power plant that makes him function as a man, a man who becomes disoriented so that he no longer knows who he is or why he is here and where he is going, cannot possibly get along with his neighbor, with other people.

That is why we are making a tragic mistake in American society. We think that the issues in our world boil down to black and white, or Democrat and Republican, or East against West, or socialism or com-

[6]Genesis 4:9.

munism against democracy. These are not the issues. The issue is man against man. Because a man who does not know how to get along with God and does not know how to get along with himself can't possibly get along with his brother. That is why Jesus Christ showed He was the master psychologist when He said, "Love your neighbor as yourself." What Jesus was saying is that the man who doesn't know how to get along and love himself cannot possibly love his neighbor. The man who doesn't know how to get along with himself, the man who doesn't love himself, has a neighbor who is in trouble.

Look at us. After hundreds of thousands of years of human history, people still do not know how to live together. We still can't bring an end to war. We still can't feed the hungry. We still can't put roofs over the heads of the poverty-stricken. We still can't learn what it means to relate to each other.

And so, mental problems have developed. Man has become neurotic—or worse.

Instead of man going to God and saying, "All right, God, I have become unplugged from You, I have detached myself from You, I have detached myself from the source of life, I no longer function as the complete man You intended me to. What is the way back to You?" Instead of man asking God this question and seeking to find a way to bridge the gulf that separates him from his Creator, that separates him from his brother, and separates him from himself, he has sought to climb back to God in his own way.

The Bible says that the sons of men built a tower.[1] Through their own strength and energy, through their

[1] Genesis 11:4–5.

own independence, through their own effort, they were going to try to climb back to God. They were going to try to find their way back to the heavens. You know the story of Babel. It ends in a confusion of tongues and they are unable to understand each other.

You can't take a man who is not plugged in, a man who does not have the spiritual life in him, who has detached himself from the power source, and expect him to find his own way back to the source. If that man is ever going to be plugged in again, someone will have to pick up the socket and put it back in the wall; someone else will have to do it, because a man can't do it himself. A depraved, separated man cannot reconcile himself to a holy God.

Today we have a lot of Towers of Babel. People think they can climb back to God through church membership. Everybody is religious, everybody goes to church, everybody has his name on some church roll. But this has not solved our problems. While we've got steeples and church buildings going up all over the place, in the name of trying to get man back to God, man still faces the same crisis. He still does not know what it means to walk with God, get along with his brother and relate to himself. Religion will not get a man back to God.

Instead of man going to God and saying, "All right, God, I have become detached from You, and as a result I can't get along with my brother," he tried to reconcile himself to his brother. He came up with sociology, social psychology, and a thousand and one studies from society, to try to understand his neighbor so that he could reconcile himself to him. If you go to the nearest library, you will find hundreds of books on social relationships, brotherhood, how to get along with your neighbor, the study of family life, the study of school life, industrial human relations and all the rest. With all these studies, through which we know more about each other than we have ever before known—we can put everyone into categories; computers can predict within one percentage point who they are going to vote for; we can even line people up and pretty well judge what kind of underwear they are wearing—we still do not know how to relate to each other, we still do not know how to get along. We still can't bring an end to war. We still can't bring an end to racism, hate and division. We still can't stop our cities from burning.

Instead of man going to God and saying, "Now look, Lord, I don't even understand myself. I don't know how to relate to myself. I'm all messed up on the inside," man tried to figure himself out apart from God. He came up with psychology, psychotherapy, and a thousand and one therapeutic practices to try to understand himself. Psychiatrists are having a field day trying to help man discover where he has come from, why he is here and where he is going. In 1967 more than 21,325 Americans took their own lives; they simply copped out because they no longer had a reason to live, they weren't able to put life together, they weren't able to discover themselves. Statistics show that the professional group that had the highest suicide rate in our country was the psychiatrists—the very people who are supposed to be dealing with the neuroses of the rest of us.

These are the crises we face in our time, simply because man decided to detach himself from the life of God.

Now the question you would raise is: "Why should what one man decided to do way back in the farthest regions of time affect us today in the twentieth century?" It is very simple. When man unplugged himself from the source of life and made himself independent of the life of his Creator, death occurred in him—spiritual death took place—and he passed that spiritual death on to every person born after him, so that each generation has been infected with this sickness of independence, and all of humanity faces the issue of identity, of community, of power.

People said, first, that you could solve the problems of these individuals—these people who don't know who they are—simply through economics. "Most people who have an identity crisis don't have enough of the good things of life. They are generally the poor, oppressed, disenfranchised people of society."

Sociologically, this is true to an extent. But it is not the complete truth. They say that the reason a kid throws a Molotov cocktail in a store window or takes potshots at the police, or rebels in other ways against the society in which he lives, is because they have locked him away from the economic rewards of their various institutions.

But if that is true, how do you reconcile the identity crisis of the kid just a couple of miles south of the ghetto, on the nearest college or university campus? This kid comes from an upper-middle-class home; his father runs the system. But he, too, is saying, Let's burn it down. And when they arrest him after he has camped in the administration building and destroyed the file cabinets, after he has tied and gagged the dean and cut the telephone lines, and taken up weapons in an attempt to stand off the state troopers from the top floor of the administration building, they discover he's got Carte Blanche, American Express and Diner's Club cards in his pockets, he's got charge plates for the major department stores in town, he was driving a T-Bird when the average poor kid was trying to buy his first bicycle. Yet he, too, is trying to destroy the system.

Economics can't be the whole answer. The two of them are passing each other on the road. As they meet halfway, the rich kid says to the poor kid, "Where're you going?"

The poor kid says, "I'm heading toward the system. You people have locked me out for four hundred years, and now I am on my way to get a piece of the action."

The rich kid says, "Well, let me tell you something, fella, I just left the system; my old man runs it, and it's a bad scene." Why is that rich kid copping out on society, why is the suicide rate among his friends increasing, why is he turning to assorted sex experiences and drugs? Because he hasn't been able to orient himself. He doesn't know who he is, and money hasn't helped him.

The second thing they said was that we need to educate people. "Education will put our society back together. Education will help people discover who they are. Education is the answer to the race problem. Education is the answer to the economic problem."

But look at our society. Since 1940, we have given ever-increasing importance to education. We are turning out thousands of people every year with degrees behind their names, competent specialists who are

going into every kind of area you can think of—
science, economics, politics. But it hasn't made our
world any better. According to the Harvard Business
School, over $10 billion was stolen in government and
industry. Who stole that money? Poor people, uneducated people? You've got to be kidding! An uneducated person would not know how. That money was stolen
by people who knew what they were doing, by people
who had access to the financial centers of power.

We are told by an independent management study
that the Pentagon wastes billions of dollars a year
through mismanagement. Here are people who are
educated, who have access to current management
techniques, who have all kinds of books and records
and films and tapes available to them to teach them
how to run a business, and yet those billions are mis-
used—simply because of mismanagement. The war was
started by educated people. Corruption in government
and industry are created by educated people. Homes
that end up in divorce courts belong to educated people. No, education is not enough.

The third thing they offered was religion. People said
that if we could make our society religious, if everybody had a creed to believe, a song to sing, a flag to
wave, we would solve our problem. We are a religious
society. The majority of the people in our country belong to one religion or another; they have their names
registered with one church or synagogue or another. If
by religion we mean that which a person believes is of
ultimate value and on which he acts, then one could be
a Communist, a Buddhist, a Hindu, a Baptist, Method-
ist, Presbyterian, Episcopalian, Catholic, Jew, or anything else you want to name, and be religious.

And yet, with all the religious activity and fervor in the world today, people still haven't been able to solve the problem of who they are, why they are here and where they're going, how they're going to relate to their neighbor, and where, in all the world, they're going to get the power to pull it off.

The black man has to learn that the white man's solutions do not work. The black man has to understand that the entire world faces the same kind of crisis that he now faces, with one big exception: in terms of social, economic and political control, the white man is in the driver's seat. But in terms of moral and spiritual dilemma, in terms of corruption and depravity, black and white sit in the same boat.

The big question that man faces is how is he going to get back to God, how is he going to get back to his brother, how is he going to discover who he was and is?

Of course, the big dilemma in terms of God is how could God, who has already said that if man became independent he would die, provide for a dead man the opportunity to live again? God began to teach His people that they could not find their way back to Him in their independent state. Somebody outside them would have to die in their place, somebody would have to take away their independence, somebody would have to put to death their independence. But this person must himself be a dependent man, must be an individual who has walked the earth totally plugged into God and, at the same time, understands what it means to be a man.

The book of Job, the oldest book in the Bible, gives

us some clue to the anguish of humanity at this point. As Job lies flat on the ground with worms eating away at his body, having lost his prosperity, his health and his wealth, he cries out to God for a mediator, somebody in the universe that might understand him; somebody that understands what it means to be a man, somebody that understands the limitations of a man, somebody that understands the suffering of a man. But, at the same time, somebody that understands the holiness and the sovereignty of God; who can take Job and his human limitations by one hand, and God and His holiness by the other and bring them together.

The prophet Isaiah picks up the lamentation and takes it through to the sixty-fourth chapter of Isaiah, where he cries out for God to "rend the heavens" and send someone down or else they will all perish. The Bible tells us that in the fullness of time, in the appointed economy of God, in the planned program of God, God decided to do something about the situation. God decided to become a man. So that we read in the first verse of John, chapter 1, "In the beginning was the Word, and the Word was with God and the Word was God."

If the idea had stopped there, my reply would have been, "So what!" But about a dozen verses later, the Bible says, "And the Word became flesh." In other words, God put some skin on Himself; God decided to come down where we are.

The Word refers to Jesus Christ, the second person of the Godhead. And the Bible says that He was one with the Father "before the foundation of the world."[3] So that even before there was a who, a where or a

³John 17:24.

what, this person, Jesus Christ, was one with the Father. You get an inkling of that when you hear God say, "Let *us* make man."[9] The plurality of God. Again, the Scripture says, when referring to Jesus Christ, "through whom also he created the world."[10] John himself says (1:2-5) that nothing was made without Him. "He was in the beginning with God; all things were made through him, and without him was not anything made that was made. In Him was life, and the life was the light of men. The light shines in the darkness" —and the darkness was not able to stop it.

And that light, that life, the eternal Son of God put some flesh on Him and came to earth in order to identify with our humanity. He came in answer to Job's cry for a person who could be limited by the same limitations that God had imposed upon man but who at the same time could understand the holiness and sovereignty of God and bring them together. And now, for the first time, God in human flesh walked the face of the earth in the person of Jesus Christ.

Of course, there are debates about that—that is, whether He was really the Son of God, whether Jesus Christ was the person who came to take away the sin of the world. What we've got to do is distinguish Jesus Christ from every other person who has ever walked the face of the earth. He's got to be different. He's got to be the antithesis of what humanity has been. That is why St. Paul refers to Him as "the last Adam."[11] You see, the first Adam had goofed. The first Adam shook his fist

[9]Genesis 1:26.
[10]Hebrews 1:2.
[11]I Corinthians 15:45.

in the face of God and told God to get off his back and leave him alone. The first Adam said, I will be my own god. I will stand on my own two feet, the captain of my own soul and the master of my own fate.

This "last Adam," this last man, Jesus Christ, has got to undo what the first Adam has done. He has got to be the complete opposite of the first Adam. The first Adam was an independent man. The last Adam, therefore, must be a dependent man; he must never once make a move independent of the life of His Father. So we must check out the life of Jesus Christ for the years that He walked the face of the earth and see if He can pull it off. If He can pull off living every moment of every day of every week of every month of every year without once ever making a move independent of the life of His Father, who sent Him, He has integrity. He can be believed. He can be trusted.

But that is not the only reason He has come. He has not only come to show us what the perfect man ought to be. He has not only come to show us what God intended man to be from the beginning. He has also come to die. He had to come to take away the independence of humanity. He had to come to take away the sin of the world. He had to put to death the death that you and I are born with. And He would not be worthy to take away our independence unless He could walk the face of the earth without ever once being independent Himself.

And, sure enough, as you follow the life of Jesus Christ, He never makes an independent move. He never really does anything. In reality, you see, Jesus Christ never really healed the sick, never really raised the dead, never gave sight to the blind, never performed any miracles. He never really did anything; His Father did it all in Him. That is why Jesus Christ says, in essence, I have come not to do my own will, but the will of my Father, who sent me. Again, He says, I do only those things which please the Father. And again He says, Don't believe Me just because of the miracles I perform, believe Me because the miracles I perform My Father performs in Me. If you ever see Me do something that My Father is not doing in Me, you don't have the right to believe Me. But as long as I am doing that which My Father is doing in Me, you had better believe Me. A dependent man.

When He told a lame man to get up and walk, He did it in the strength of His Father. When He told a blind man to see, He did it in the strength of His Father. When He told a dead man to get up out of the grave, He did it in the strength of His Father. And when He spat on the earth and made clay and applied it to the eyes of a blind man so that the blind man saw, I suggest to you that He spat in the energy and strength of His Father.

That is why, if you check out the temptations that Jesus Christ faced, you see that He was never asked to do anything grossly immoral. Jesus Christ was never asked to kill anybody; He was never tempted by the devil to start a war or go out and commit adultery or fornication or anything like that. But He was tempted to act independently of His Father, because that is what sin is. Sin is being your own god, saying you can stand on your own two feet. And what Jesus Christ decided to do was set aside those prerogatives that were His as the Son of God, and to set aside all the powers

that He had with the Father before the foundation of
the world, in order to become limited by the same limitations that He, as God, had imposed upon man. That
is why, you will notice, Jesus Christ never did anything
in His own strength. As God He had the strength and
the power to raise the dead, to heal the sick, to give
sight to the blind, to do all the miracles He performed.
But He never once used His own power. He always
derived everything He did from the strength and energy
of His Father. That was why He was perfect; He never
made a move without His Father.

You will notice, in the first temptation He faces in
the wilderness after His baptism, that the devil comes
to Him and asks Him to do a ridiculous thing. After
Jesus has fasted forty days and forty nights, the devil
says to Him, If you are the Son of God, command that
these stones be turned to bread. Now I ask you, what
in the world is sinful about making bread out of stones?
Absolutely nothing. Then why would the devil tempt
Him with a ridiculous thing like making bread out of
stones? It is very simple. The devil was saying, in effect, You are hungry. You haven't eaten in forty days
and forty nights. You are the Son of God; therefore,
You've got enough God in You to be like God without
God. Why don't You simply make bread out of those
stones on Your own, in Your own power? Use Your
own strength as the Son of God; don't consult Your
Father.

You see, if he could get Jesus to make just one
move, such as a simple thing like making bread out of
stone, and get Him to do it in His own strength, Jesus
would have sinned.

It was because Jesus was perfect, because He never

once made a move without His Father, that the Bible declares that He was worthy to bear in His own body our sin. He was worthy to put to death our independence, because He was a dependent man.

And so the Bible declares that when this person, Jesus Christ, was arrested—supposedly for insurrection and blasphemy, claiming that He was the Son of God; indeed, co-equal with God—and when they laid that cross upon His shoulders and forced Him to bear it to a place called Calvary, He was not simply bearing on His shoulders a wooden cross but, the Bible teaches, He was bearing upon Himself our sin, our independence. And it was really this that He shrank from when in the Garden of Gethsemane he prayed, "My Father, if it be possible, let this cup pass from me; nevertheless, not as I will, but as thou wilt."[12] What was the cup that Jesus feared? Was it death? No, He was no coward; He had come to die. Was it crucifixion? No, crucifixion was a common form of execution with the Roman government. Then what was it that He shrank from? It is the fact of suffering, the suffering He would have to endure. And I don't mean here the physical suffering, although there was much physical suffering involved—when arrested, they beat Him, they mocked Him, they spat upon Him, and then they took and laid on His shoulders this cross and forced Him to bear it all the way to Calvary, beating Him along the way. This was not the suffering He shrank from.

When they got to the place of execution they took the cross and laid Him on top of it. Then they took long Roman spikes and drove them through His hands and feet. And while the spikes were being hammered

[12]Matthew 26:39.

into His body, the soldiers were digging a hole in the ground where the cross was to be placed. The cross was lifted up and dropped into that hole; and as it was dropped into that hole, the cross vibrated and the spikes ripped through His flesh. They ripped through His hands and through His feet. That was pain; that's physical hell. But that was not what He shrank from. It was the fact that, as He hung on that cross, the Father with Whom He had fellowship before the foundation of the world—His Father Whom He said had sent Him, and by Whom He did everything; the Father Who performed all the work in Him; the Father with Whom He had done such fantastic wonders—now would turn His back on Him, leaving Him all alone. This is why Jesus Christ cried out, "My God, my God, why hast thou forsaken me?"[13]

You see, at that moment, God the Father had turned His back on His only Son. And the reason is that at that moment Jesus Christ was experiencing hell; He was experiencing separation from God—simply because He was being made sin for you and me. When God looked down on that cross, He no longer saw His Son, He no longer saw the perfect Lamb of God; when He looked down on that cross He saw you and me and all of our depravity and our independence from Him. The holiness of God cannot look upon sin; the holiness of God cannot hold fellowship with sin. The Scripture teaches us, "He made him to be sin who knew no sin, so that in him we might become the righteousness of God."[14] On that cross Jesus Christ literally experienced

[13]Matthew 27:46; Mark 15:34.
[14]II Corinthians 5:21.

the hell that you and I deserve for being unplugged from the source of life. He experienced the hell that should have been ours because of our independence from Him. And when Christ died on that cross, He took our independence and put it to death. Someone has well expressed it when he said that, on the cross, Christ killed death dead. He took our place; He died in our stead.

Christ took our independence—our urge to produce hate and envy and jealousy and all the other sources of conflict and indifference in our world—and nailed it to the cross. Once and for all, He was saying, I am putting to death the human race; I am putting to death the first Adam and all that the first Adam accomplished which separated man from God, man from man, and man from himself. I now put it to death; I now kill it. I now destroy it by My death. This is what He meant when He said, "It is finished"[15]—I have finished off independence; I have finished off the human race that was born in the first Adam; I have finished off the thing in man that produces lust and greed and hate and racism.

But another thing happened on that cross. The Bible says that Jesus Christ shed His blood.

Now all the way back in the early books of the Bible, we read that life is in the blood—that is, life is in the bloodstream of man. Jesus Christ shed His blood on the cross, which means that He shed His Life. And we read that His blood was shed in order to cleanse us of every sin that we have ever committed, to cleanse us of the result of our independence from God, to cleanse our lives. We read in the Scripture where it says "and

[15]John 19:30.

the blood of Jesus his Son cleanses us from all sin."[16] We read again in the Scripture that "therefore, we are now justified by his blood."[17] Again, the Word of God says, "If we confess our sins, he [God] is faithful and just, and will forgive our sins and cleanse us from all unrighteousness."[18] And that cleansing comes through the blood of Jesus Christ.

So not only did Jesus Christ die to kill death dead, not only did He die to kill off our independence—the thing in us which produces sin—He also shed His blood so that we could be cleansed and forgiven. The word used in the Bible is "justified." And as you break this word up, you'll get its meaning. Just-if-I'd—Just as if I'd never sinned. In other words, the blood of Jesus Christ was shed to make it possible for you and me to stand in the presence of God just as if we had never sinned. If racism is ever going to be dealt with, and if any other sin of humanity that causes violence is ever going to be dealt with, and if injustice and inequality are ever going to be dealt with, we have got to deal with the thing in man that produces sin and apply to it, by faith, the fact that Jesus Christ shed His blood to cleanse us of our sin so that the guilt of the past can be washed away and man can start a new relationship with God, with his brother, and with himself.

But it is not enough merely to have my independence put to death or to have my acts forgiven. If I am going to be the man God intended me to be, if I am going to walk the face of the earth as God made man

[16]I John 1:7.
[17]Romans 5:9.
[18]I John 1:9.

to walk—in other words, if I am no longer going to be like the first Adam was but, like the last Adam, if my life is going to be like that of Jesus Christ—I must get the power to pull it off. Which is why, the Bible says, three days later Jesus Christ got up out of the grave.

Upon that statement, that Jesus Christ rose from the dead, rests the whole possibility for redemption and regeneration in human society. When Jesus Christ got up out of the grave, He said, "All authority in heaven and on earth has been given to me."[19] In other words, all the power of heaven and earth was now committed to this person Jesus Christ. He didn't rise from the grave just to prove that He had power over death, but so that if people would dare to trust Him and commit their lives to that radical, revolutionary, resurrected Christ, that same Christ would come inside them and live His life through them. He would make it possible for them to live in a hostile world with their two feet planted on the earth as a living testimony that it is possible for an invisible God to make Himself visible in Christ through human flesh.

That is why, when Jesus Christ rises from the dead, the Bible refers to Him as "the second man."[20] The first Adam failed, and it took the last Adam, the Lord from heaven, to live His life in total dependency upon His Father so that He could be worthy to die on the cross and put to death the works of the first Adam. The first Adam is gone; the last Adam has been crucified. And now Jesus Christ rises from the dead, no longer as the last Adam, but as the second man—a new man, the

[19]Matthew 28:18.
[20]I Corinthians 15:47.

leader of a new creation. The Apostle Paul said that "if any one is in Christ, he is a new creation; the old has passed away, behold, the new has come."[21]

When Jesus Christ was nailed to the cross, He put you and me on that cross with Him and finished us off. That's what the Apostle Paul meant when he said in Galations, chapter 2, verse 20, "I have been crucified with Christ": When Christ was nailed to the cross, I was nailed to the cross; when Christ was put to Death, Tom Skinner's sinful nature was put to death; when Christ was nailed on the cross, my independence was nailed on the cross with Him. When Christ shed His blood, He shed His blood to forgive me for the results of my independence. When He arose from the dead, He made it possible for me to be a new man by coming inside of me and living His life in me. "The old has passed away, behold, the new has come."

Jesus Christ emerges not only as a great religious leader, not only as a great moral and ethical teacher, but as the leader of a new creation, a revolutionary who gets to the root of man's problem. He destroys that in man which produces independence from God, and then, as man is willing to trust Him, He comes in to live His resurrected life in him and makes him radically new.

That is the gospel—that is what it is all about. When we talk about the gospel of Jesus Christ, that is what we mean. Man was created with a choice of being independent or dependent. He chose to be independent. When he did, he died. His independence separated him from God, his brother, from himself. Then Jesus Christ, as the last Adam, came to undo what the first

[21]II Corinthians 5:17.

Adam had done by living His life in total dependency upon His Father, and because of that He was worthy to bear in His own body our independence and to die in our place, to experience the hell we deserve. When He shed His blood, He shed His blood to cleanse us, to justify us and to forgive us. And when He rose from the dead, He made it possible, if we would dare to trust Him, to live in us. That is the gospel. It is the only message that will redeem society.

IV The Workability of the Gospel

If you ask, "Tom, how does that work, how can it become relevant to my personal life, how can I be sure all you say that the gospel is theoretically can be applied to our everyday lives?" The way that I must answer is to say it has worked practically through my own life.

I was born and raised in Harlem, that 2½-square-mile area in uptown Manhattan with a population of one million. On my block were four thousand people. Forty-six percent of the kids in my community born since 1945 were born out of wedlock, and 57 percent grew up without their fathers, producing what the sociologists call a matriarchal society—which simply means that the kid's old man wasn't home. In that context, I tried to discover who I was. I tried to solve the problem of identity, the problem of my neighbor, the problem of power.

I knew that I was black, and I knew that I lived in a black community. But I didn't know who I was.

I watched television to try to find a life pattern that would give me an inkling as to my identity. But I saw none. Oh, yes, they had Rochester on, Jack Benny's sidekick, who always came out saying "Yes, boss" and

"No, boss." People tried to tell me that was me, but I said, No way! I thumbed through the various magazines and newspapers to try to find something that related to me, but I found nothing; generally, when a black man ends up in the news, it is because of something illegal or immoral he has done. When I started school they gave me a grade-one reader. It had stories about Dick and Jane and Sally and a dog named Spot who said "Bow-wow!" They were all white with the exception of Spot—they integrated him.

As I grew older and came under the influence of people in the Harlem community who began to teach me about my history and my past, I realized how even the educational system had gypped me out of my blackness. I soon discovered that the history books in school didn't tell the truth about my people. I hadn't learned, for instance, that the man who first put his foot on the Arctic Circle was a black man, or that the doctor who first performed heart surgery in America was a black doctor, or that the doctor who founded the blood bank in America was a black doctor, or that the inventor who first patented the type of shoe we wear today was a black man, or that the man who helped lay out Washington, D.C., was a black man.[1] All of this had been left out of my history books. I soon began to get very angry as I developed a concept of my own blackness. (You've got to keep in mind that this was

[1]Matthew Henson, Peary's assistant, planted the U.S. flag at the North Pole in 1909. Dr. Daniel Hale Williams performed an open-heart operation in 1893, and Dr. Charles Richard Drew established blood banks during World War II. Jan Matzeliger patented a lasting machine in 1883 that halved costs of producing shoes. Benjamin Banneker served on the commission that surveyed our future capital in 1791.

long before the "Black Is Beautiful" slogan. Those of us in Harlem knew we were black long before people came along advocating "Black Is Beautiful," "Black Power" and all the rest, so that I never suffered from a problem of "blackness.") But I soon discovered that merely knowing I was black, even though I was convinced that black is beautiful and all the rest, still did not help me discover altogether who I was.

The person who doesn't know how to get along with himself can't possibly get along with people. This frustration led me to join one of the up-and-coming gangs in the Harlem community. Six weeks after joining I defeated the leader in a knife fight. For two years, I led the Harlem Lords in rioting, looting and stealing, and every imaginable type of violence and immorality you can think of. I could bust a bottle over a fellow's head and be undisturbed about it; I could take a bottle, break it in half, jig the glass in his face and twist it without batting an eye. I ended up with twenty-two notches on the handle of my knife, which meant that my blade had gone into the bodies of twenty-two different people—and I didn't care. All that mattered to me was to get what I wanted; how I got it made absolutely no difference.

All this came to a climax one night while I was planning strategy for a gang fight. This was to have been the largest gang fight in the city of New York. While mapping out my strategy, I had my radio on, listening to my favorite disk jockey, a rock 'n' roll program which came on every night between the hours of eight and ten o'clock. Normally at nine o'clock there was a station break, a commercial, and the disk jockey returned with the rest of the program. But on this particular night, instead of the disk jockey returning to the air, an unscheduled program came on.

For one half hour a man spoke from a passage written in Second Corinthians, chapter 5, verse 17, which says, "Therefore, if any one is in Christ, he is a new creation; the old has passed away, behold, the new has come." And the speaker went on to preach the essence of the gospel.

He said that the whole reason Jesus Christ came to earth was for the purpose not only of living a perfect moral life but of bearing in His own body the sinful nature I was born with—my independence. He went on to describe Jesus Christ in a new way for me.

I had turned the whole concept of Jesus Christ off; I had written Christianity off as the white man's religion, given to the black man in order to keep him in his place. All the pictures I had seen of Jesus were of a docile kind of individual, an Anglo-Saxon Protestant Republican. He was soft and effeminate-looking, with nice smooth hands that looked as if they had just been washed in Dove. I rejected Him on the ground that, if that was Jesus Christ, we could beat Him up on any street corner; He looked too soft to walk my neighborhood after dark. The impression I had of Jesus from the white society that preached about Him was as the defender of the American system, president of the New York Stock Exchange, head of the Pentagon, chairman of the National Republican Committee—a flag-waving, patriotic American—and against everything else. The impression I had gotten from these people who talked about Jesus Christ was that He was anti-Catholic, anti-liberal, anti-Communist, anti-everything.

For the first time, I began to see that the Christ

which leaped out of the pages of the New Testament was no docile, effeminate, passive individual, but rather a tough revolutionary radical; a man's man, with hair on His chest and dirt under His fingernails. The kind of Christ who could look the establishment in the face and say, "You brood of vipers!"[2] He said, in essence, You hypocrites! You filthy sepulchres, you're like dead men's bones!

Does that sound like soft language to you? He was a Christ who could wrap cords around His hands and walk into the temple where they had desecrated the worship house of His Father, and He could knock over the money counters and drive out the money changers and the cattle and, standing there in holy anger, say, "It is written, 'My house shall be called a house of prayer'; but you make it a den of robbers.'"[3] Does that sound like a softy?

Yet He was a Christ Who could be filled with compassion, a Christ Who could weep over a city, a Christ Who dared rub shoulders with the common people, Who sat and ate and drank with prostitutes and drunkards and harlots and thieves; He was a Christ Who was so compassionate that He could look at a woman in the gutter who had been caught in adultery and tell her that her sins had been forgiven. But, again, a tough Christ Who wouldn't tolerate injustice and inequality.

There was no way I could respond to an effeminate Christ. I could understand why He was pictured the way He was. The people who drew these pictures lived out in suburbia. They didn't know about the inner city;

[2]Matthew 3:7, 12:34, 23:33.
[3]*Ibid.*, 20:13.

they didn't know about Harlem; they didn't know about the ghettos, the slums, the rats and the roaches. The Christ they needed was a Christ Who could pamper them, a Christ Who could put a nipple in their mouths to pacify them, a Christ Who could help Johnny get gas from his old man so he could drive the car over the weekend; they needed a Christ Who could change their diapers and take them to the bathroom and wipe their tears.

The Christ I needed was a tough Jesus, a Christ Who could help one live with the anguished cry of a mother whose two-week-old baby had been gnawed to death by a vicious rat or burned alive in a fire caused by faulty wiring, a Christ Who could help fight both the landlord who refused to provide services in that slum building, while collecting excessive rents, and the corrupt housing inspector who would palm $100 and never report the violations. I needed a Christ Who could help me live through paying 25 percent more for food at the supermarket in my neighborhood while making 48 percent less than white society, a Christ Who could help me cope with the flourishing narcotics and numbers rackets in the community which were supported by the local police. That was the kind of tough radical Jesus I needed, and that was the kind of Christ I heard described that night, the kind of Christ Who had died in my place.

But I had a problem. Everything that preacher said he quoted from the Scripture. And in my opinion the Bible was a nice, poetic, religious history book concerned with the dealings of some supreme Being and the superstitious people who had the audacity to believe that He existed.

I had grown up with the religious bag—that is, I had grown up in the black church. I had seen and understood the culture in which Christianity was preached. Let me clarify what I am saying. The black church is the most powerful social institution in the black community. It has been the only place that black people could have power and exercise control without white intervention. It was here that we played politics and economics, and all the things that we were not able to do in the wider society. That is why for almost every member of the church there was a club or organization.

Jesus Christ is historically the scapegoat for the white man. Black people have always identified themselves with the children of Israel, in bondage in Egypt, always praying for the Moses who would deliver them. "Go down Moses, 'way down to Egypt land, and tell old Pharaoh to let my people go." Many of the songs that developed out of the black churches were based not only on theology but on the condition of slavery. "Steal away, steal away, steal away to Jesus." A slave might sing that song in his cabin as a signal to the underground railroad, meaning, "Harriet Tubman and the underground railroad are coming through tonight and I'm stealing out of here." Or when he sang, "Going home in a chariot in the morning," he might mean, "By morning time, I'm gonna be gone." I understood that.

I also understood the power struggle that went on in the black church. Whoever was head of the church in the black community was head of its most powerful social institution. Out of this situation came much hypocrisy, much fighting for power. James Baldwin sums it up when, referring to his boyhood preaching, he says:

Being in the pulpit was like being in the theatre;
I was behind the scenes and knew how the illusion
was worked. I knew the other ministers and knew
the quality of their lives. And I don't mean to
suggest by this the "Elmer Gantry" sort of hypocrisy concerning sensuality; it was a deeper, dead-
lier, and more subtle hypocrisy than that, and a
little honest sensuality, or a lot, would have been
like water in an extremely bitter desert. I knew
how to work on a congregation until the last dime
was surrendered—it was not very hard to
do—and I knew where the money for "the Lord's
work" went. I knew, though I did not wish to
know it, that I had no respect for the people with
whom I worked.[4]

Having grown up in the church most of my life, my
reaction was very much the same, because I knew the
hypocrisy, I knew the games that were played, I knew
that for a great number of black people the church was
just an escape from reality, and that the preacher knew
this and played on their fears and superstitions. I had
been to enough tent meetings to see the evangelist who
came through selling his blessed handkerchiefs or
blessed water.

But the preacher who preached that night, as I lis-
tened, quoted a verse from John, chapter 6, verse 37,
where Jesus Christ says that "him who comes to me, I
will not cast out." Either that was a lie or that was the
truth, and there was only one way to find out: go to
Him, give Him my life, surrender myself to Him. If He

[4]Baldwin, *The Fire Next Time* (New York: Dial Press, 1963)
pp. 51-52.

didn't work, I could tell God to get off my back and go hang Himself. I would have no way of knowing unless I experimented, unless I put God to the test.

I bowed my head next to the radio that night and prayed a very simple prayer. "Lord, I don't understand all of this, I don't dig You and I don't understand where You're at in my life; but if these things are true, then I give You the right to take over my life." At that moment, Jesus Christ, the Son of God, took up residence in me.

I had no emotional, traumatic experience. I saw no blinding flashes of light. No thunder roared, and no mountains caved in. I felt no tingling running up my spine. I just accepted the fact that, if God is God, God can only be God because He doesn't lie, and Jesus Christ, who is God, said the person who comes to Him He will not cast out.

The first reason why I know He took up residence in my life is that my life has never been the same since that night. My whole life took on a radical new direction. I didn't become an angel overnight, and I didn't all of a sudden put the whole thing together. But my life began to take on new direction. For the first time I had a sense of purpose, I had a sense that I belonged to the God of heaven and earth, I sensed that God's Word was true—Jesus Christ was now in me and my sins were forgiven, not the sins that I committed as a black man, but the sin that was mine as a human being: to be born in the human race without the life of God.

The second reason is because from that moment on I have not had to make any effort to be a Christian. I had always been under the impression that the Christian life was a struggle, that in order to be a Christian you carried in your inside pocket a list of rules and regulations: Don't do this. Stay away from that. Don't touch the other. And, for God's sake, don't look at that! That you went out and broke your neck trying real hard to be a Christian. You adjusted a halo around your head and held yourself real tight, hoping that you wouldn't slip, always afraid that God, the "super cop," would bust you if you made the wrong move.

That idea has been especially detrimental to black people. For too long they have been hoodwinked into believing that they have got to struggle for something, some unattainable goal. This was the method the black pastor used to keep his black congregation in subjection. He was always telling them that they had to come out to the meetings because they must have good attendance. The black preacher was worried about the size of the congregation for a number of reasons, but mainly because of the offering to be taken up. The collection would pretty well determine his own salary, and determine, from a status point of view, whether his church would compete with the other black churches in the community. But he would always tell the people, "You've got to come out in order to work out your soul's salvation." He made them feel that if they didn't attend they would lose their salvation. He made them feel that only if they worked in the church and followed the program of the church and were obedient to the church's demands and gave the amount of money the church had figured out they ought to give, would they be able to make it into the Kingdom. And there was what we called the "holiness" crowd. They said that if you wore earrings or lipstick and face powder, or if you didn't have your hair cut right, or if you weren't clean-shaven, you weren't going to make it into the Kingdom.

For the first time I began to see through my relationship with this person Jesus Christ. The Christian life was not my attempt to be like Jesus; rather it was Jesus being Himself in me. I have learned that I cannot be a Christian and that God doesn't expect me to be one; that's why He died for me, that's why He shed His blood, that's why He rose again from the dead, so that He could live His own life through me, without any assistance from me. I have learned that God doesn't need my help in order to be God; all He needs is my availability to Him. I have learned that the Christian life is Jesus Christ doing His own thing in me, instead of me trying to do my thing. And the exciting thing about it is that Jesus Christ has been perfectly capable of being Jesus Christ in me without my help.

In the black church I use to hear that much-heralded phrase, "God helps those that help themselves," and I used to think that you had to go out and give God some assistance in order to be a Christian. That's not the case.

I went back to my gang and told them I had committed my life to Jesus Christ and walked out without being touched. I have had the privilege, since then, of leading several of the other fellows to an understanding of Who Jesus Christ is.

What has this done for me personally? Well, now that Jesus Christ lives in me, I know who I am—I'm a son of God. This doesn't mean that I have negated my blackness. I want to make this very clear. The gospel of Jesus Christ is black in the sense that it does not ask a black man to give up his blackness in order to be a

Christian. If there is one existing myth that I will fight,
it is the myth that a commitment to Jesus Christ means
one has to develop a "white mind." We must distinguish between the white culture, which has penetrated
the black community in the name of Christianity, and
what the Bible teaches as being Christianity. What the
Bible teaches as being Christianity and what the white
culture has made Christianity are two different things.

I have not had to negate my blackness in order to be
a Christian, but rather, now that I am committed to
Jesus Christ, it is God's desire to live His life through
my "redeemed blackness." I'm God's son; I'm a member of the royal family of God, which puts me in the
best family stock there is in all the world, which makes
me better off than the Queen of England's kids and the
kids of the President of the United States. All the
Queen of England's kids can say is that their mom is
the Queen of England. But, you see, my Father is the
God of heaven and earth; I'm a member of the royal
family of God, which means that I can now go out and
face the world with a completely different attitude. I
am secure in who I am; I am a black man in whom
God is living. I no longer have to be ashamed. I have
discovered what I always knew, but in a very real way
now. Black is beautiful, but a lot more than that, a lot
more beautiful, since Jesus Christ is living through it,
and one of the things I have discovered is that Jesus
looks great in black.

My being God's son makes God responsible for
looking after me. He is obligated by our son-Father
relationship to take care of me. My security is now in
Him, and therefore it is much easier for me to deal
with my white pagan friends. I no longer approach

them with a sense of inferiority; neither must I bear hatred of them in my heart in order to feel superior. The black brother is right at the point where he says that we must see ourselves as men, we must recognize that we are not inferior, we must no longer see ourselves as second-class citizens—he is right at that point. But often, because of his own independence from God, having to deal with another independent pagan, he has to hate the man in order to feel superior to him. My commitment to Jesus Christ—now that I am God's son—means that I don't have to do this; I don't have to hate my white friend in order to prove to him that I am secure. Neither do I have to change his attitude toward me. So often we measure ourselves by what other people think we are. If other people think we are inferior, we either see ourselves as inferior also or we become very angry. But I know who I am, whether others know it or not. Therefore, I can simply be myself.

This does not mean that I am not committed to justice, to the black man's struggle, to the black revolution, because I am. Anybody who has observed the social scene, anybody who knows what's going on, knows that the black revolution—in the sense of seeking to obtain economic, social and political power, rectify injustices, eliminate poverty and exploitation of people in the black community—is a just cause. The difference is that I no longer go out and fight for dignity for myself because I already have it, as God's son. I am now engaged in a fight against injustice, a fight against social inequality. But as God's son, I've got to obey God's word. And the book of Micah says, "What does the Lord require of you but to do justice, and to love kindness, and to walk humbly with your God?"[5] So I become involved in boycotting the chain store in my neighborhood, which is charging 25 percent more for food than is charged in the white community just south of me, because that is unjust, and the justice of the Kingdom of God, to which I belong, demands that I do something about it. I become involved in rent strikes, in my building, or anybody else's building, where people are being exploited and where the landlord is not providing services for the people, because that is a matter of justice. As a member of the Kingdom of God, I've got to obey my Father, who seeks to deal with injustice. I am involved in trying to get the schools in my community decentralized so that black kids will be able to go to school with black leadership and grow up understanding that there are leaders who are black, so that they can learn something about themselves, so that the people in the black community will have some control over their political and social and economic destiny, because that is a matter of justice. Not because I am out for anything personal; I am out to rectify injustice—be it black or white—as a member of the Kingdom of God.

The difference is that, as God's son, my fight must be based on the principles of the Kingdom of God. I do not have to hate my white brother or my white friends while demanding justice. I do not have to be at the point where I want to kill him. In other words, I am willing to go out and fight, willing to give my life to rectify unjust causes, but I am not going to become unjust myself in the process. Because I am God's son

[5]Micah 6:8.

Secondly, not only do I know who I am, I know what I've got. The Bible tells me that I am not only God's son but also a joint heir with Jesus Christ. This means that, with Jesus Christ, I will inherit everything that God has. The Bible says that I am a partaker with Jesus Christ of every spiritual gift in heavenly places. All that is acceptable to Jesus Christ is acceptable to me, which makes me the richest person in all the world. I don't mean this in terms of dollars and cents but in terms of the spiritual wealth that it takes to make a man a man. What makes a man a real man is his ability to love, his ability to be at peace, his ability to be patient, his ability to be temperate, his ability to have mercy—his ability to have all the "fruit of the Spirit" that we read about in the fifth chapter of Galatians.

As a black man I faced not only my intense hatred for the white man but also my inability to get along with my black brother. You see, I had been so brainwashed and so filled with hate and bigotry that if a black brother tried to stand in my way I wanted to eliminate him too. We've got to face the fact that this hatred exists today in the black community. After having to go out and work five or six days for the white man, after being cheated and exploited by him day after day, by Friday night, or Saturday and Sunday, we've gotten back at each other. My Connection with Jesus Christ has not only given me the security of knowing who I am, it has helped me to understand who my neighbor is and how I should respond to him, and it has given me the power to do it.

All the love that it takes to be a man, all the patience that it takes to be a man, all the sensitivity that it takes to be a man, all the mercy and all the joy and all the temperance that it takes to be a man, is mine in this person Jesus Christ.

There are some who would say, That sounds like a softy, that sounds effeminate. No, it doesn't. You must remember that those are the characteristics of Jesus. While He was tough, He was peaceful; and while He was tough, He was loving; and while He was tough, He was full of mercy; and while He was disciplined, He was patient. And because I know I am connected with Jesus Christ to inherit everything that God has, I do not have to cut my brother's throat to try to get ahead, I don't have to step on him or play the "house nigger" role, seeking always to outdo my brother in order to impress my white pagan friends. No, because now that I am connected with Jesus Christ, I have a sense of security, not only as to who I am but what I have, a sense that God guides my destiny, that I belong to Him, that my now and my future is His. Therefore, I can deal with my brother. I can deal with my black brother and my white brother with a sense of security. I can fight justice without having to worry about the repercussions. I can love my enemy without having to worry about being taken. Simply because my destiny is controlled by the God of heaven and earth.

And three, the Bible tells me, in the book of Ephesians,[6] that I am seated together with Jesus Christ in the heavenly places, which puts me on the highest social level in all the world. I swing with Jesus Christ and company. I don't have to break my neck to belong to any particular social group, because I am already on the highest social level.

Now don't get that mixed up with operating in the

[6] 1:20.

social world. I'm not talking about belonging to a white or black society in terms of education and economics. I am talking about wanting to rub shoulders with a particular group of people simply for the prestige involved. I do not want to send my daughter to a particular school simply because a certain class of whites or a certain class of blacks attend that school. If the school happens to be the one where my kid is going to get the best education, I want her in the classroom because of the education involved. I want the right to hold a certain job because I am qualified to hold it, not for reasons of prestige. I want to hold that job as a matter of justice, as a matter of principle.

Knowing who I am, what I have, and what my position is because of Jesus Christ changes my reason for being involved in the black revolution. Because of my relationship with Jesus Christ, I am not involved in the black revolution simply because I want to replace an existing system. I am involved in it because there are areas in the system that are diametrically opposed to the Kingdom of God, and that which is opposed to the Kingdom of God, I must oppose as God's son.

So I know who I am. I am a black man in whom Jesus Christ is living. A black man with his two feet planted on the earth who has the privilege of having the God of heaven and earth living in him. A black man committed to the black revolution not to negate the existing system but because the black man's cause is a just cause, based upon the principles of the Kingdom of God. I am not interested in overthrowing white society any more than I am interested in allowing white society to overthrow black society. I am interested in overthrowing injustice. I am interested in dealing with inequality. I am interested in setting wrongs right. Because those are the principles of the Kingdom of God.

I must be involved in the struggle for justice whether it concerns a white man or a black man. If a black man's rights are being denied, I must be committed to his fight because it is a matter of the Kingdom of God. If a white man's rights are being denied, I must stand against my black brother in order to rectify that wrong because it is a matter of the Kingdom of God. I am not involved in the black revolution simply because it is "black"; I am involved in the black revolution because it is Christ.

I have solved the problem of community. The gospel of Jesus Christ solves that problem. I now know who my neighbor is: He is any person I come into contact with, he is all the people of the world. And my attitude toward my neighbor has definitely changed because I know who I am. A man who knows who he is can certainly get along with people.

My attitude toward my neighbor is: Because Jesus Christ is alive in me, all I ask is to love you. Whether you love me back or not is unimportant. I can now derive enough love from the life of Jesus Christ to be able to survive without your love. But what I do ask for is the privilege of loving you.

When I say this, I am talking to both white and black brothers. I've got to be able to love my white brother, even though he's exploited me, even though he might be filled with injustice, even though he is born and raised with cultural prejudices, even though he might be out to take me. Because I am now a member of the Kingdom of God, I have got to love him. But just because I love him does not mean I will allow him to walk all over me; it does not mean that I will not stand against his injustice; it does not mean that I will not fight him at the point of inequality. But in doing so, I will do it with love and compassion and always in an attempt to reconcile him to me and to my Savior.

There must also be love for my black brother. When a black brother talks about "we've all got to get together, and we've all got to love each other as black brothers and sisters," he is generally talking about that love on his own terms. A large number of black brothers, for instance, consider the message that I preach and the gospel of Jesus Christ to be counterrevolutionary. Therefore, they put people like me on a list for elimination when the revolution comes. So I've got to love my black brother, too. I've got to love my black brother who is always out to out-black, always trying to prove that he is blacker or tougher than the next brother. I've got to love the black guy in my community who is nothing but bad news, who feels, because of his frustration, that any black man who seems successful has got to be eliminated. I've got to love the black brother who hasn't learned to stop beating his wife, who hasn't learned to come home to his children, who hasn't learned to stop drinking up 70 percent of his salary at the bar—all in the name of getting back at "Charlie." I've got to love the white brother who made him like that, who presses him five or six days a week and forces him to live in a rat trap.

But I have got to have the kind of bold, courageous love that makes it possible for me to look my black brother in the face and tell him he has no right to beat his wife, no right to drink up his salary, no right to be filled with bitterness and frustration when there is deliverance for him. Jesus Christ said he had come "to proclaim release to the captives . . . to set at liberty those who are oppressed."' I've also got to have the courage to look my white exploiting friend in the face, and, like Jesus, call him one of "a brood of vipers," tempered with the kind of love that, if he is willing to repent, I am open to be reconciled to him. That is my responsibility to my neighbor.

I now have the power to pull it off. In me there is the living Christ; in me there is the very power of God Himself. The Bible tells me, "Christ in you, the hope of glory."' The Bible again says that "he [Jesus Christ] who is in you is greater than he who is in the world."' Philippians, chapter 1, verse 6, says that "he who began a good work in you will bring it to completion at the day of Jesus Christ." First Thessalonians, chapter 5, verse 24, says, "He who calls you is faithful, and he will do it." It other words, for everything that God asks me to do, for every demand that God makes upon me, for every command He gives me, He is available in me to turn around and do it through me. This makes Jesus Christ exciting! This makes the Christian life vibrant!

So I have solved the problem of identity, the problem of community, and the problem of power. The gospel of Jesus Christ is relevant to the black man's condition. It is relevant in liberating that man. It is relevant in showing him what his responsibility is.

I firmly believe that if America is ever going to have a spiritual awakening, if it is ever going to be the kind

'Luke 4:18.
'Colossians 1:27.
'I John 4:4.

of nation where the Spirit of God is operating, this is
only going to come as people are willing to submit
themselves to obeying the teachings of the Scripture.
And perhaps the person best fitted to head that kind of
spiritual revolution in America is the black man.

The reason for this is that the oppressed has always
had a greater sense of righteousness than the oppressor.
The white man, by his exploitation, by his cultural
hang-ups and limitations, by his institutionalized racism, has devalued the coinage of moral and spiritual
leadership in the Western Hemisphere. The time may
well have arrived for the black man to carry the ball. If
so, he can make this his finest hour or he can waste it
in a haphazard attempt to get reprisal and reparation
through violent revolution—which won't work. We not
only have the opportunity to fight inequality and injustice, we not only have the opportunity to fight those
wrongs which so engulf our nation in shame and dis-
gust, we also have the opportunity to provide leadership. And I suggest that we can only lead when we do
what the white man has failed to do in all these years—
and that is to make ourselves totally available to this
Christ Who died in our place, Who shed His blood to
forgive us and rose again from the dead to live in us.

I can immediately hear some objections. I can hear
some say, Yes, but the black man has been singing and
praying and trusting Jesus for generations; he has been
down on his knees crying out to God, and God hasn't
delivered him—in fact, it has been his belief in God
that has kept him back; this is the very weapon the
white man has used to keep him down.

Let's keep in mind that while the white man has used

his Christianity to exploit people, you can't blame God for that. And while it is true that there were large segments of the white community which twisted the Bible in order to maintain the slave system, and while it is true that slavery was upheld by the church as a divine institution ordained by God, Jesus Christ never identified Himself with those actions. He was never a part of that. Those were pharisaical, religious hypocrites, who themselves were not really committed to the truth of God's Word, who had never allowed Jesus Christ to be Lord of their lives, but who simply took the religious subculture and used it to maintain and perpetuate their own particular economic and social ends.

You must also admit that it was the penetration of the truth about Scripture that not only sparked within the black man his desire for freedom but motivated him to fight for it. One of the greatest "mistakes" the white man made during the years of slavery was to teach certain slaves to read, and the one book that was read most often was the Bible. There is no other book in all the world that rings with more pride for liberty and justice and freedom and equality. That is what the folksinger meant when he said, "There is a book, and every page rings liberty." Harriet Tubman led more than three hundred black men to freedom through the underground railroad. When she was asked by what means she did it, by what authority she got the right to become involved in leading so many people out of slavery, she stood up and quoted the very Scripture that Jesus Christ quoted in the temple: "The Spirit of the Lord is upon me, because he hath anointed me to preach the gospel to the poor; . . . to preach deliverance to the captives, . . . to set at liberty them that are bruised."[10]

All those people who argue that the message of Jesus Christ has been used to hold black people down are not right. It is true that there were those who twisted the message of the Bible to hold black people in subjugation, but the real message of Jesus Christ—that which speaks of Christ Himself—and people who stood firm in preaching about Him as Lord, kindled fires of freedom and helped bring about the end of slavery. Many of the abolitionists of those early days spoke out as a result of a spiritual revival that came about through the preaching of the Word of God, from the New Testament. The Word of God spoke out against slavery and struck the conscience of a freedom-loving people, the Word of God restored sanity to our people through those dark days of exploitation, the Word of God was the symbol of freedom and justice and equality.

If black people throw out the one weapon that has sustained them for all these years, if we throw away, in this hour of revolution, the one book that has been our guiding light, we are throwing away truth—and there can be no real revolution without truth. Jesus Christ Himself said, "I am the way, and the truth, and the life; no one comes to the Father, but by me."[11] If we do not then deal squarely with the truth, personified in Jesus Christ, if we do not follow His way for Living, for true revolution, for real radical change, His way to be real men and real women, His way to the leadership that our country is in dire need of—if we throw away His truth, which is the person Jesus Christ, our

[10] Luke 4:18 (King James Version).
[11] John 14:6.

revolution goes the way all other revolutions have gone. If we throw away the Word of God, and the testimony of God through His Son, Jesus Christ, we throw away the life; and we fall into the same trap as our oppressor.

While religion has been part of the institutional establishment, it has been a religion without life. True life comes through Jesus Christ; no man is really alive without Him.

This could be the black man's finest hour, if he could bring to the social, economic and political revolution, a spiritual revolution. For the spiritual revolution precedes all other revolutions; it cannot come later. As the Bible says, "Righteousness exalts a nation, but sin is a reproach to any people."[12]

I have not always been involved with Jesus Christ like that. I have not always been committed to Jesus Christ like that. There was a time when I thought Jesus Christ was a nothing. When I heard about Jesus, I discovered that He was just a carpenter, a man who had banged nails into wooden planks. I checked out His education and I was sure He was nothing. He'd never been to any institution of learning, He had no degrees behind His name, He had never studied at the feet of any of the great philosophers. I did not commit myself to Him because academically He didn't have what it took. He was a nothing. I looked at His dress, and I found out He went around in the dress of common people. He didn't dress in fine linen. He was a nothing.

I pictured Him as a schizophrenic religious leader, so obsessed with Himself that He wanted everybody else to be obsessed with Him. They tried to tell me He was the Son of God, and I decided He was a religious nut. They tried to tell me that He was born of a virgin, and I figured that at best He was an illegitimate child.

And then one day I met Him. I encountered that Christ, and I was overwhelmed by Him! I saw Him as the God of heaven and earth, and I committed my life to Him. I now know Him and I count Him to be superior to anything that men can offer. Because of my commitment to Him, I count my family name as garbage, my economic status as garbage, my social position as the dung hill of Jerusalem, that I might know Him and be found in Him. Not having my own righteousness, that I might be discovered in Christ with the righteousness of God. My commitment to Him, my ambition, is to please Him, and to allow Him to flesh Himself out in my black body.

I submit to you that if we can get a glimpse of that kind of commitment in the twentieth century, we can shake our world. May I ask you a personal question? To whom are you committed? Is Jesus Christ more important to you than name? Is Jesus Christ more important to you than family status? Is Jesus Christ more important to you than economic security? Is Jesus Christ more important to you than social status? I will challenge you that there are many of you who are very much dismayed with evangelical Christianity—to the extent that some have copped out on it. And I can't blame you. But what is your alternative? What are you going to replace it with?

I'm simply suggesting that if the evangelical church is irrelevant today, and I believe it is, and if the evangelical church is stale and archaic and impractical, and I believe it is, then the only way we're going to correct it is to return to the Christ of the New Testament. We need to return to that masculine, contemporary, revolutionary Christ who leaps out of the pages of the Bible to call men to Himself. It is only by virtue of our relationship to Him that we're going to change the church structure and make it relevant to the twentieth century.

You will not solve the problem by turning your back on it. You will solve it by returning to the Christ upon whom the church was supposed to have been built in the first place, and allowing Him to be Himself in you, so that you can go out and shake your world.

I wonder if God has spoken to you about being totally committed to Him with no strings attached. Are you prepared to make that commitment to become Christ's revolutionary in the twentieth century? Just say to Jesus Christ, "Lord, here is my life. I give You the right to do with me whatever You please; I give You the right to run my life, and I'm prepared to cut the umbilical cord to anything in order to be totally attached to You, to take my orders directly from You, so that people might in me see You. I'm prepared to be available. I'm prepared to make the sacrifice. I'm prepared to be as radical as You are prepared to be in me. But I'm prepared to let You also be Lord and Master. I'm prepared to take my hands off my life and to stop trying to be what You want and to let You be it for me. I'm tired of trying to be a Christian and getting frustrated with other Christians who are in the same bag. I'm prepared now to be delivered from that bag, to let You be Yourself in me."

All you have to say is, "Lord, I believe that."

V Jesus Christ the Radical

Many people seem to think that the message of Jesus Christ negates the black revolution and that one has an either-or choice: either be committed to the black revolution or be committed to Jesus Christ. There is no either-or choice, because Jesus Christ Himself was a revolutionary. And Jesus Christ is not out to negate the black revolution. If an individual commits himself completely to the Lordship and authority of Jesus Christ, it does not mean that he cops out on the black revolution; it just means that he is involved in the black revolution with a new direction, with a new spiritual and moral perspective, and with a new Master.

In the mind of Jesus Christ it was never a question during His day as to whether or not there was going to be a revolution; it was just who was going to lead it. And the question in our day is not whether or not there is going to be a revolution. There is going to be a revolution; there is no possible way by which this country, with all of its years of intense hatred, slavery, and racism, can possibly free the oppressed people of this generation without revolution. The question is, What kind of revolution will it be and who is going to lead it?

When Jesus Christ walked the earth over nineteen

hundred years ago, he found Himself caught in a revolution, a revolution that was very similar to the one we are involved in today. The Romans were exploiting the Jews. A Roman could give a Jew his baggage and tell him to carry it for a mile, and the Jew would have to do it without pay. A Roman could walk into a Jewish home and tell the owners he was staying there, and there was nothing the family could do about it. A man who tried to protect his family might lose his own life.

There arose a band of radical people: Jewish rebels who decided that there was only one way to deal with the Romans, and that was to fight them on their own terms, with violence. Jesus had a couple of these Zealots in His own group. Judas was one; Judas hoped that Jesus Christ would set up His kingdom here on earth and overthrow the Roman Empire, setting up the Jews as the ruling class of the world. Peter was another; Peter felt that there was only one way to deal with the Romans, and that was to cut them down. Peter was ready to fight; he felt sure that with all the power Jesus had, His fantastic ability to perform miracles, combined with His attributes as being the Son of God, He was going to put those Romans down. You'll remember that it was Peter who first went for his sword at the Garden of Gethsemane where the soldiers came to arrest Jesus.

At this particular time in history, there was a Jewish radical by the name of Barabbas. Barabbas had formed a band of guerrillas, and Barabbas said to his people, There is only one way to get that Roman honky off your back, and that's to burn him out. The only thing the Romans understand is fighting fire with fire. We've got to deal with them on their own grounds. So Barabbas and his group of guerrillas made themselves Molotov cocktails and threw them into those nice Roman homes—and they burned. Barabbas led his band through the countryside, ravaging one Roman house after another, intimidating one group of Romans after another. They would pillage and rape and kill and murder. Barabbas became a threat to the Roman establishment, and they arrested him.

In those same hills was another radical. His name was Jesus. Jesus didn't have any guns or ammunition, Molotov cocktails or tanks; He had no band of guerrillas. He went around preaching about a thing He called the Kingdom of God. Now, in essence, Jesus would have agreed with Barabbas concerning the Romans. Jesus would have said, Barabbas, you're right, the Roman system is exploitive; it is malicious, materialistic, filled with murder and hate and graft and corruption, and the group of people are polytheistic and pagan. But Jesus would have also said, Barabbas, when you burn the Roman system down, when you have driven the Roman out, when the Roman Empire loosens its grip on our people, what are you going to replace the system with?

It would not have been enough for Barabbas to have answered Jesus by saying that the important thing was for the system to go down. You've got to have a complete program; if you are going to tear a thing down, you must know how to replace it. Jesus would have perhaps challenged Barabbas; this is what made Jesus so radical. He not only questioned the system, He also questioned the motives of the people who were fighting the system. Jesus would stand up, with no qualms about speaking against the injustice and the inequities of the establishment, and He would tell the establishment off. But He would also stand up to those people who wanted to tear the establishment down. Jesus was always getting at the root cause of things.

For instance, there was the man who came to Jesus and said that his brother was cheating him out of his birthright. Obviously, the man had a good case, his brother was cheating him. Of course, Jesus would have addressed Himself to that. But He took the opportunity, while the man was standing there griping about his brother cheating him out of his birthright, to question the man about his own motives. He said, in effect, Look, are you anxious to get your hands on that money because of your covetousness, or do you really want to deal with the situation because of its inequity? He said to the man, Beware of covetousness. In other words, "Your brother is wrong, but so are you. That's what made Jesus radical. He never took sides; He always dealt with the right or wrong of a situation.

So Jesus would have said to Barabbas, Barabbas, you're right, the Roman system stinks. It's corrupt to the core. But you are going to tear it down with your own corrupt nature; and in the name of getting rid of corruption, you are being corrupt, and you are going to replace the Roman system with your own messed-up kind of system. (In the process of killing off the Romans, Barabbas was also killing off Jews who didn't agree with him.)

This reminds me of some of the brothers in the black revolution today. They tell us, "We've got to get rid of the society. The Man is corrupt; the Man is exploiting us; the Man is on our back." They are right; but then they become exactly like the Man they want to get rid of. They tell you that if you don't agree with the way they plan to carry out the revolution you have to be eliminated too. They are not only interested in getting rid of "Charlie," they are also interested in getting rid of their own black brothers in the name of being a revolutionary.

Jesus would say that there was no way He could buy that. "Charlie" is wrong, but if you are going to become like "Charlie," you're wrong, too.

Now, Barabbas, He would say, there is no difference between a Roman leech and a Jewish leech; there is no difference between a Roman murderer and a Jewish murderer; there is no difference between a Roman thief and a Jewish thief; there is no difference between a Roman rapist and a Jewish rapist. So that I have not come, Barabbas, to take sides. I have not come to be on the Roman side or the Jewish side. I have come as the Son of God to establish a new Kingdom, a Kingdom that starts by radically transforming the lives of people, and all people whose lives become transformed because they commit themselves to Me, and allow Me to become their life, become members of the new Kingdom on earth and on their way to heaven.

That message was potent, so powerful was this radical Jesus who addressed Himself to the establishment and had the audacity to address Himself to the reactionaries and rebels in His own group, who were acting very much like the establishment in the name of getting at the establishment. He was a Christ that was so tough and so disciplined, and yet so filled with compassion and love and mercy, that a tax collector put down his books and followed Him, a Jewish rebel put down his sword and followed Him—Matthew, the tax collector, was definitely a member of the establishment; Peter, a Jewish "militant," had been ready to lead the Jewish underground at any time.

It is only at the cross of Jesus Christ, it is only through Jesus Christ, that the Stokely Carmichaels, the Eldridge Cleavers and the Rap Browns can hold hands with the Whitney Youngs and the Roy Wilkinses. It is only at the cross of Jesus Christ that a left-winger and a right-winger can surrender their particular political idiosyncrasies to become committed to the Kingdom of God. It is only at the cross of Jesus Christ that a black man and a white man can stand together.

Thousands of people started following this person Jesus Christ. The Bible says that the common people heard Him gladly. So radical was He in His preaching that people came for miles and miles to hear Him and to see Him. Word went out that this was the Messiah, this was the Son of God, this was the One whom the prophets had spoken about. Great throngs of people followed Him. The lame started walking, the blind started seeing, homes were put back together again; people who were corrupt got straightened out and thieves started living right; Roman soldiers, the throngs in town, and the radicals started getting converted, and the revolutionaries and the Uncle Toms of the establishment started getting together around Jesus.

Jesus too, became a threat to the Roman establishment, and so they arrested Him.

There were now two revolutionaries in jail, Barabbas and Jesus. It was around festival time, the governor, Pilate, stood up before the Jews in town and said, in effect, Look, it is festival time and at this time of year I'm supposed to release a prisoner. I've got two prisoners in jail. Whom shall I release to you? Should I let this one go? His name is Jesus. I don't find anything much wrong with Him. He claims to be the Son of God. I've examined Him and find Him to be basically an innocent man. But He is accused of inciting the people; He is accused of blasphemy. I've also got Barabbas, here, who is a murderer, an insurrectionist, a rebel who's been burning the system down. Whom shall I release to you, Jesus or Barabbas?

With one voice the people cried out, "Barabbas!" Pilate was doubtless stunned by such a choice. It wasn't Jesus who was burning the system down. He was not the threat to their homes, to their children and their family. He was basically an innocent man. They also knew that Christ had healed some of them, that Christ fed some of them, that Christ had put some of their homes back together, and there were lame people and blind people and deaf-and-dumb people among them who were walking, seeing and hearing because of Him. But they cried out for His blood. Why did they want Jesus crucified and Barabbas released?

There were two reasons. One was that if Barabbas went free and he started some more trouble—that is, if he rounded up another band of guerrillas and started intimidating the establishment—they could always call in some more troops to put his revolution down; just call out the cops or the state troopers or the national guard and they'd put Barabbas down. But how do you stop a man who doesn't have any guns; how do you stop a man who doesn't have any Molotov cocktails; how do you stop a man who's got no tanks, no ammunition, no army, no fortress, no underground hideout, a man who lives His life like an open book? How do you stop that kind of man, who just speaks a word and the blind see, who doesn't have to be in a man's house to say "Heal" and a man is healed; how do you stop a man who is getting revolutionary results and doesn't use revolutionary weapons? How do you stop a man that without firing a shot has gotten more people following Him than Barabbas had with all his guns and ammunition? How do you stop a man who is peaceful and loving, and yet tough and hard-nosed and disciplined? They felt that the only way to get rid of Him was to crucify Him.

The other reason they didn't want Jesus was because of the demands His revolution would make upon them. He laid down some plain facts. If one was going to be His radical, His revolutionary, Jesus said in Matthew 16:24, "If any man would come after me, let him deny himself"; if any man is going to be My disciple, let him give himself up, "take up his cross and follow me." That was hard. It meant a person had to give up what he wanted, his personal ambitions and desires and needs, in order to follow the Lord from heaven, Who's got no money in His pockets and Who doesn't want to sit on anybody's throne but His own—and His Kingdom you can't even see. That was too demanding.

People can't understand that God's way and man's way are different. Man formulates his own ideas about how a revolution should take place, and if God doesn't fit into his plans he wants to down God.

This is precisely what some of the brothers are saying now. They are saying that if you are going to trust Jesus Christ, how can you be involved in the kind of revolution that is going to get "Charlie" off your back? They don't understand that any man who becomes committed to Jesus Christ becomes a member of the family of God, and God becomes obligated to look after that individual. They say, "Yeah, but I know a whole lot of black people who have been exploited while trusting Jesus," and they miss the point. The point is simply that no person who is committed to Jesus Christ or who follows Jesus Christ is ever really exploited—not really. The person who is committed to Jesus Christ is always in command. And wherever God would have him, he is there to speak to the system in the name of Jesus. Jesus had said to those people who wanted to be His radicals, "If any one comes to me and does not hate his own father and mother and wife and children and brothers and sisters, yes, and even his own life, he cannot be my disciple."[1] By that Jesus meant that those people who would follow Him should have love for Him that is so intense that all other loves in their lives seem like hatred by comparison. This was just too much for the people. To be willing to love Him above father, mother, sister and brother, husband or wife, and even one's own self was too much to take.

They were willing to accept the benefits He offered. They were willing to accept the fact that if He would overthrow the Roman Empire and set up a kingdom, they would hang with Him in order to get a stake in that kingdom. But to pay the price in order to belong to His Kingdom, to love Him more than any other in their lives, to swear their allegiance and loyalty to Him to the exclusion of themselves, was too much.

This is the real reason why people today don't want Jesus Christ: They would basically have to give up themselves. It is not so much that those leading the

[1]Luke 14:26.

black revolution feel that Jesus Christ is counterrevolutionary (which they can't possibly believe that if they
read the Scriptures); rather, it is the allegiance He demands, the idea that one must give up his own personal
aspirations and desires, that is the real issue. People
don't want God to be in charge. They want to do their
own thing instead of God's thing. And so they simply
say that Jesus Christ is the white man's God, or they
write Him off by saying He's counterrevolutionary,
even though in their own consciences they know this
couldn't possibly be true if they read history. They just
really don't want Him because He demands their all.

Jesus also says in the fourteenth chapter of Luke
(verse 33) that "whoever of you does not renounce all
that he has cannot be my disciple." Jesus was saying, If
you want to be my radical, if you want to be my revolutionary, I demand that you leave behind all you've
got, that you take all that you are and all that you have
and totally commit it to all that I am. That's what He
demands. That's what it means to be a true radical.

This was too much for the people to take, and so
they cried out, "Crucify him."[2] Get rid of Him; get
that man off our hands. Let His blood be upon our
children and upon our children's children. But get Him
off our backs.

And so they crucified Him. They took Him and
nailed Him to a cross, and they thought for sure they
had gotten rid of Him, and they laid Him in a tomb
and rolled a stone across its entrance. They wiped their
hands and said, That takes care of that revolutionary,
that man who pricked our conscience, that man who
dared to struggle against the establishment, that man

[2]Mark 15:13-14.

who dared to demand our allegiance. He's off our backs now, and we can go and do our own thing. We've gotten rid of that radical.

But what they didn't bargain for was that three days later, Jesus Christ pulled one of the greatest political coups in all of history. He got up out of the grave. No other radical has ever done that; no other revolutionary has ever done that. There has never been a revolutionary leader who was able to give up his life for his followers, die in their place, experience hell for them, and then come back from the grave to lead them—and not only to lead them but to live in them, to make them new, to establish a whole new radical kingdom, a whole new army of men totally committed to him. So radical was His resurrection, and so radical was His impact on the lives of the many who dared to trust Him, that those bands of Christians, those bands of people called His disciples, went out and, according to the words of their own critics, "turned the world upside down."[3] They shook the world.

The Roman Empire was never the same. It made such far-reaching impact upon the society that one man on his throne shook and trembled. And on one occasion when a preacher stood in front of him and told him all the truth about Jesus Christ, he rocked and cried out, "Enough, enough! I've heard enough! In a short time you think to make me a Christian." The impact of those young radicals of the first century who had committed themselves to Jesus was so devastating that emperors thought the best thing to do was to get rid of them, so they threw them into arenas where wild

[3]Acts 17:6.

animals had been starved for weeks, and these Christians were eaten alive.

To save themselves, all they had to do was to promise they would never again mention the name of Jesus; they would never preach His word, they would never open their mouths about Him, they would never swear their allegiance to Him. But they refused, and they were eaten alive. Others of them were nailed to crosses, where straw was lit under their feet and their bodies were burned to ashes—simply because they would not renounce their allegiance to Jesus. Others were tied to stretching stakes, and their bodies were stretched until every ligament and bone was ripped apart—and all they had to do to prevent it was promise never to swear their allegiance to that radical, Jesus.

But for every one that died, ten more rose to take their place, and they shook the Roman Empire with words and deeds and the life that was available from the Lord of heaven.

In the midst of the black revolution, that Jesus is available to help us shake America to its very roots—a shaking that America has never known in all its history of racism and religious hypocrisy, its commitment to words and deeds in a constitution that has never really been fleshed out in everyday life. America needs a radical revolution. Revolutions cannot be effective if they are merely economic, if they are merely social, if they are merely political; they've got to be spiritual and moral, they've got to shape people from the inside, they've got to transform the very structure of a man, because what a man is shapes what he does. That is why the Bible says that as a man thinks in his heart, so is he.

If you want to change society, you have got to change the way people think. Only Jesus Christ the radical can do that.

VI The Results of the Gospel

This radical band of men known as the disciples of Christ shook their world; they turned it upside down. They did this because, the Bible says, they were filled with the life of Jesus Christ—that is, these men lived in such a vital relationship with Jesus Christ they were intoxicated with God. Keep in mind that they preached the truth about Jesus Christ in an exploitative, dictatorial, totalitarian Roman state; some of the very same men who swore allegiance to Jesus Christ had at one time committed themselves to spending their lives trying to overthrow the Roman Empire. It was not that the Roman Empire no longer needed to be overthrown, not that it wasn't totalitarian and dictatorial. They simply discovered that they could address themselves to the issues of the Roman Empire and at the same time be committed to the principles of the Kingdom of God. But they were committed to the principles of the Kingdom of God first.

What were the ingredients, what were the results, what proved that these men were intoxicated with God? I am convinced that in the midst of the black revolution we face today, it is not that the American system doesn't need to be changed—it does need to be changed, radically—and anybody who observes the social scene cannot overlook the fact that our country is entrenched with racism and political, economic, and social corruption. In fact, no one needs to look at the various laws that are on the books to recognize that many of the laws of our land serve only special-interest groups; we do not need to look past the recent events that have taken place in government to recognize that the group of people who contribute the highest amount to the political campaigns at the times of election can often control the appointments of various men. So we do not argue the point that the system needs to be changed. We know it does.

But what I am saying is that to try to attempt changing that system without a radical change in the fundamental nature of man is a futile revolution. And I am saying that what our country needs is a revolutionary leader (who in God's providence could well come out of the despised black community itself), a man intoxicated by God; and that it will take men of God—men who are filled with the life of Jesus Christ—to go out and lead the political, social and economic revolution in the name of God. Which is really what the early disciples did.

I'd like to share with you the results in the lives of men who were intoxicated with God, the results of the penetration of the common clay of man's humanity by the gospel of Jesus Christ. In the third chapter of the book of Acts, Peter and John are on their way up to the temple to pray. There is seated at the gate of the temple a man who has been lame from birth, a man who has never walked in his entire life. This man sits at the gate of the temple holding out his hands to beg for money. People would drop a few coins in his hands as they went up to the temple to pray. In other words, all these people did was make this man comfortable in his misery; no one had ever made an attempt to deliver him from his misery. They would put some money in his hands and go on to the temple to pray and rejoice, and have what they call a "good time in the Lord," and take great pride in the fact that they were "the last of the Mohicans," holding on to truth; that while everyone else was denying the truth about God, while all the pagans were denying the existence of God, they were the last of the faithful, remembering the true and living God; and they'd come out of the temple after their prayers and rejoicing and walk right past that lame man sitting by the temple.

This reminds me of the twentieth-century church in so many ways. It goes back and forth, praying and singing and rejoicing in the God that it claims to pay its allegiance to, walking past a lame world. Perhaps the thing concerning the gospel of Jesus Christ that has turned people off, especially in the black community, is that so many who have named the name of God have paraded back and forth past a crippled people, 10 percent of their number, the most powerless, moneyless group of people in the country. Occasionally they would drop a few coins in the cups of black people and say, "The Lord bless you." There has sometimes been a little tokenism, a few handouts and government programs, all in the name of pacifying "those" people; but they have never really done anything about their crippled condition.

As Peter and John were on their way up to the temple to pray, the man held out his hand to beg money from them. So Peter said, "Look at us. . . . I have no silver and gold"—we don't have any money, we are broke—"but I give you what I have; in the name of Jesus Christ of Nazareth, walk."[1] And the man got up and walked.

What Peter and John were saying was simply this: For three and a half years, we have walked with a man Who lived His life in total dependency upon His Father. He never once made a move without His Father, and because of this He was perfect. That Christ, Who made Himself available in Him to do everything He wanted. And that Christ told us that as He lived by His Father, so we, if we depend upon Him, shall live by Him. Just as He was available to His Father, His Father was available to Him. We have made ourselves available to Him, and He is now available to us. And because we are available to Him, He is alive in us, and in His name, in His authority, we tell you to get up and walk. And the man walked.

This is what the relevancy of the gospel of Jesus Christ must be—and is—to the black community. The gospel of Jesus Christ must say to a community that is economically powerless, that is politically powerless, that is socially powerless—to an exploited people, to a people who are stepped upon, a people whose past is filled with anguish and sorrow—the message of Jesus Christ must say and does say, "Rise up and walk!" The church must get involved no matter what the cost; and not only in preaching that message but practicing it.

When the lame man walked, the miracle of that healing spread through Jerusalem and became the talk of the town. But for anything God does which is spec-

[1]Acts 3:4, 6.

tacular—any time God is working through the common clay of man's humanity; any time God has turned somebody on so that now that person is available to God and begins to behave like God's man—there are always critics.

Verse 13 of chapter 4 in the book of Acts says, "Now when they saw the boldness of Peter and John, and perceived that they were uneducated, common men, they wondered; and they recognized that they had been with Jesus." In other words, the critics looked at Peter and John, and they turned their noses up and raised their eyebrows and said, "These are a bunch of ordinary men. They don't speak with a cultured accent, they have not been to any of the institutions of learning that we've been to, they've got no degrees behind their names, they don't swing with the crowd we swing with, they aren't dressed in linen and purple the way we are, they're dressed in common marketplace clothes, sheepskin and goatskin." And so they laughed at them.

But the Bible says that when they saw the confidence and the boldness of Peter and John, when they looked at these men and saw the very countenance of God being reflected in their lives, they knew that they had been with Jesus.

When a man has something to do with God (a man who is intoxicated with God, a man for whom the gospel has begun to work in his life), that man will reflect the life of Jesus Christ, that man will show that he has been with Jesus.

This was a shock to those first-century Uncle Toms because, you will remember from the last chapter, they were the ones who collaborated with the Roman Empire to get rid of Jesus. And they thought they got rid of Him because they saw Him nailed to a cross, they saw Him buried. Oh, yes, they got word that the grave was empty and that Christ was supposed to be resurrected from the dead, but they weren't going to buy that; they explained it by saying that the disciples came and stole His body. They were not about to believe that Christ is alive. But when they looked at Peter, they saw Jesus. When they looked at John, they saw Jesus. God had come alive in the common clay of their humanity. And that shocked the daylights out of them.

This is the problem in the black community, and it is even more a problem in the white community, because often Christianity in the black community is a reflection of white Christianity. Often Christianity in the black community is dead because it is dead in the white community. When black people imitate white Christianity, they come up dead, too—on the short end of the stick. Which is why a lot of the radical revolutionary brothers tend to think that Christianity is the white man's religion, because it is as dead as their religion. They fail to recognize that you can't have a religion that is alive without the life-giving source. There was never any doubt in the people's minds about the authenticity of what Peter and John were preaching, because they looked at Peter and John and, in their very behavior, saw Christ.

I reiterate: If the black revolution is going to be effective—economically, socially, politically—if it is going to make the kind of moral and spiritual impact that it ought to make on the world, if it is going to show men how they ought to live and how they ought to lead, if the black man is ever going to teach his white brother what it really means to be moral, the leadership must come from people who are Christ's men, people who are intoxicated with Christ, people who have been with Jesus, people who reflect the life of Jesus. And that reflection of the life of Jesus is not your attempt to imitate Him; it is not your going out struggling and breaking your neck trying to be a Christian; it is not carrying a bunch of rules and regulations around in your pocket; it is not a matter of not drinking, smoking, nightclubbing, miniskirting or anything else. It is a matter of letting Jesus Christ, Who is God, live His life in you, based on your availability to Him—it is, in essence, becoming His slave.

That's the problem; they object to being His slaves. What they don't recognize is that everyone—black and white—is in slavery to somebody or something. Some people are slaves to their money, some people are slaves to their social position, some people are slaves to their family, some people are slaves to their cars or their homes, some people are slaves to their jobs.

Peter and John became the slaves of Jesus Christ, so that Christ could live through them. Even their critics could look at them and see Jesus. That's the result of the gospel. Inevitably, being with Jesus and reflecting the life of Jesus means you behave like Jesus. Your attitude toward people, your attitude toward injustice, your attitude toward poverty, your attitude toward hunger, your attitide toward the inequities of society, your attitude toward government, toward money, toward your home, toward your position, all begin to fall into place and take on the point of view Jesus Christ would have had about all of those issues.

Peter and John were threatened with their lives, and they were told never again to speak or teach in the name of Jesus. Verses 19 and 20 say, "But Peter and John answered them, 'Whether it is right in the sight of God to listen to you rather than to God, you must judge; for we cannot but speak of what we have seen and heard.' "

I would like to suggest to you, in the second place, that a person who is intoxicated with God lives oblivious to public opinion. He does not care about what people say.

Peter and John were threatened by the establishment. They were told that if they ever went out and mentioned the name Jesus—and notice, that it is preaching in the name of Jesus, that it is preaching in His authority that scared the daylights out of the Pharisees; they were getting revolutionary results, and the town was getting stirred up—they would lose their lives. Peter and John said, in effect, Listen, whether it is right to listen to you or to take our orders from God, you decide. But while you are making your minds up about it, I want you to know that we cannot help but speak of those things we have seen and heard. For three and a half years we've walked with the Lord of heaven and earth. For three and a half years we lived with a man Who lived His life in total dependency upon His Father. We saw Him nailed to a cross. We saw Him buried, and we saw Him three days later after He was resurrected from the dead. With our own eyes we saw Him ascend to heaven. If you're asking us to be quiet about that, you have got to be out of your minds!

Imagine, they are talking to the establishment, the people in town who run the show. That kind of boldness comes as a result of hanging around Jesus and being intoxicated with Him.

Oh, yes, there have been people who've been bold politically, and people who have been bold in the social world. But always keep in mind that many of them were bold because it was economically and politically expedient. They were bold when the wind was blowing their way. They were bold when they knew they had a constituency standing behind them. But Peter and John have no constituency; they are outnumbered.

Perhaps the shame of the church in the twentieth century is that it has not been bold. Perhaps the reason that we have come to this revolutionary hour, where blood may well flow in our streets, is because of the inequities and injustices and exploitation of the black man, and now because of his anger. This has had to happen because the church has not been a true church; it has not obeyed the claims of God to live oblivious to public opinion. It has proved by its very structure that it is an institution; and institutions, by their very nature, are conservative, because they must conserve what they have accumulated; and they tend to protect the society that helps them and tempts them, rather than addressing themselves to that society.

That's what has made Jesus Christ so radical. He never owed His allegiance to anybody. He didn't owe His allegiance to the Jewish radicals; neither did He owe His allegiance to the establishment or to the Uncle Toms. He owed His allegiance to the Father Who had sent Him; therefore, He could afford to address Himself to all of them in the name of His Father without worrying about the reprisals. He took His orders from His Father. This is why Peter and John couldn't be bought. They said, We've been told to take our orders from the Christ who sent us. We cannot help but speak.

Many of the problems we have today would not be what they are if people who claim to be Christians had spoken out. If those people who sign contracts saying they will never sell their houses to black people had been boldly spoken against by those who name the name of God, we would not be in this revolutionary hour. If Christian real-estate men who claimed to know God, who were going to church taking communion, had sold homes to people who could afford them, regardless of the color of their skin, we would not be in this revolutionary hour. If pastors who claim to be the prophets of God had had the courage to stand up and preach the truth to their congregation, even if it meant losing their pulpit, even if it meant that the Board of Trustees would vote them out, we would not be in this revolutionary hour. If black preachers who claimed to be the oracles of God to their people had not been living off the people's pocketbooks, constantly worrying about how big the offering was going to be, and had not always been out trying to tickle the ears of their people, trying to get folks "happy" and jumping on benches and all the rest but rather had talked the truth about God, so that we would have produced a morally and spiritually strong people who could have led this country, we would not be in this revolutionary hour!

Peter and John said, Listen, we take our orders from God, not from you. The Bible says they let Peter and John go.

In verse 23 of Acts, chapter 4, it says, "When they were released they went to their friends and reported what the chief priests and the elders had said to them." They went back to their friends. This tells me that the early disciples had a relationship with each other that was thicker than blood brothers and sisters. They didn't go back home, they didn't go back to their families, but, rather, they went back to their friends, they went back to the fellowship of believers, they went back to those other people who had become intoxicated with God.

One fundamental problem with the twentieth century is that people don't know how to be brothers; they don't really know how to be sisters; they don't really know how to relate to each other. When these early disciples shook each other's hand and addressed each other as "brother" or "sister," they really meant it. It was the kind of brother-sister relationship where they were prepared to lay down their lives for each other. They looked after each other. They cared for each other. They protected each other.

I don't take stock in the people today who go around addressing each other as "brother" and "sister" in the name of the revolution. A guy will stand up and say "That's my black brother" or "That's my black sister." And then he's ready to go out and sack out with another man's wife. If that brother's your brother, how in all the world can you sack out with his wife? If that sister is really your sister, how in all the world can you desecrate her?

There's the white brother that tells me that I am his brother and that he loves me "in the Lord." And when I move next door to him, he moves out. He tells me that I am his brother, and as soon as my five-year-old daughter starts turning his six-year-old son on, he calls him in out of the street, because he's afraid they might plan to intermarry or something. He tells me that I am his brother, but I can't worship in his church and I can't preach in his pulpit. He says that I am his brother, but he signs a contract which says he will not sell his home to a black man.

That's not the kind of relationship these early disciples had. They had a relationship that was thicker than blood brothers or sisters. "They went back to their friends," and they told the fellowship what had been said to them and how their lives had been threatened. And the Bible says, "And when they heard it, they lifted their voices together to God"[2]; they began to pray.

One of the results of being intoxicated with God, one of the results of the gospel becoming a reality in a man's life, is that he spends much time praising God, he spends much time making love to God, if you please. Someone has said, "He who would be holy must spend time with Him who is holy." You will notice that throughout the New Testament, wherever you see men who were spectacular in terms of the impact of Christ on their lives and on the society in which they lived, it was because they spent a lot of time with God. They didn't always spend that time griping to God; they spent that time praising God and reminding God of Who He was.

"Sovereign Lord, who didst make the heaven and the earth and the sea and everything in them." Then they went on to quote the Second Psalm: "Why did the Gentiles rage, and the peoples imagine vain things?"[3] They reminded themselves that this was not the first time Satan had raised his ugly heel against the people

[2] Acts 4:24.
[3] *Ibid.*, 24-25.

of God, this was not the first time that a person who is intoxicated with God had faced problems.

There are a number of people who think that a commitment to Jesus Christ, becoming filled with His life, means that your problems go away. Again, this is where some of the revolutionary brothers who don't have their theology right are in argument with those of us who preach the message of Jesus Christ. They think a commitment to God means that one's problems will go away, that all poverty will disappear, that all of a sudden open housing will take place, that all of a sudden the voters' registration drive will triple, and that all of a sudden the Ku Klux Klan will disappear and racism in America will go down the river. That is not true; no one has ever said this will happen. We are simply saying that, when a man becomes intoxicated with the life of Jesus Christ, he now has the strength and the ability to face his problems; he has the wherewithal to deal with his enemies, to go through his life without cracking up. A black Christian and a black pagan will still have to live in the same world and face the same exploitation. It doesn't mean that simply because you become a Christian the landlord is going to stop exploiting you or that "Charlie" is going to get off your back or the police are not going to be brutal any more. It simply means that you now have a built-in problem solver, Jesus Christ, Who is able to help you deal with life—His way, on His grounds, on His terms.

After they reminded themselves of Who God was, and after they reminded themselves that this wasn't the first time people who were intoxicated with God faced problems, verse 29 says, "And now Lord, look upon their threats"—Now that we are reminded of who you are, look at their threats"—and grant to thy servants to speak thy word with all boldness." They didn't ask God to remove the problem; they did not stand there and say, All right, God, get rid of the Sanhedrin council, get rid of those Pharisees, get rid of the Uncle Toms, get rid of the establishment that is holding us back. They never once prayed that.

They just reminded themselves of Who God was and, once they knew God was in control, asked that God grant to them the boldness to speak anyway. That's the difference between a leader and a coward. A leader doesn't expect his problems to go away; rather, he goes out and meets them head on. This is what the disciples were saying: Give Your servants the boldness to meet the problem head on. You have commissioned us to preach the truth about Jesus Christ, You've commissioned us to preach the gospel, You've commissioned us to feed the hungry and the poor, You've commissioned us to put clothes on the backs of the naked, You've commissioned us to put a roof over the heads of those who have none, and we are going to go out and do what You've commissioned us to do—even when our lives are threatened—and all we ask is that You give us the boldness to do it. We don't ask that You remove the problem, we don't ask that You make the problem go away, we just ask that You will give to our brothers the boldness to speak anyway.

The Bible says, in verse 31, "And when they had prayed, the place in which they were gathered together was shaken; and they were all filled with the Holy Spirit and spoke the word of God with boldness." The place was shaken. That's always true of people who are attached to the Kingdom of God: They get shaken.

God knows that in the twentieth century there needs to be a shaking in our world. This is what the gospel will do—and I mean the *real* gospel; I don't mean simply the words about the gospel, or the songs about the gospel, but the gospel, the truth about Jesus Christ, the truth about His liberating power, the truth of His ability to set men free, the truth about His ability to make His life in the common clay of any man's humanity who is available to Him. That truth will shake men; it will shake men from their complacency, it will shake men from their self-satisfaction, it will shake men from their racism, it will shake men from their prejudices, it will shake men from their corruption, it will shake men from their immorality, it will shake men from their militarism. It will shake men! And if there is anything the gospel of Jesus Christ must do in the twentieth century, it must shake men, it must shake society, it must shake institutions, it must shake the very fiber, the very core, of the existing structures in our country.

Verse 32 says, "Now the company of those who believed were of one heart and soul; and no one said that any of the things which he possessed was his own, but they had everything in common." Those who believed were of one heart. People continue to ask me what the answer to racism in America is. The answer lies in that thirty-second verse: To be intoxicated with God, to be filled with His spirit, to be a radical for Jesus Christ. The result of that radicalism is that we are of one heart and one soul. But you cannot come up with people that are of one heart and one soul if they are not committed to Jesus Christ. You cannot have a man who is committed and a man who is not be of one heart and one soul; it takes both of them, sold out to the authority and Lordship of Jesus Christ, to produce the oneness.

That one heart and one soul is across-the-board fellowship, eyeball-to-eyeball fellowship. Today there are too many people who want to have fellowship on their *own* terms. The black man wants to have fellowship on his terms, and the white man wants to have fellowship on his terms. God is saying that if you want to have real fellowship it has got to be on *Christ's* terms. Not fellowship based on paternalism, not fellowship based on your being the way I think you ought to be, not a oneness based on your compromising to meet my conditions, or my compromising to meet your conditions; but rather a fellowship based on the fact that both of us, with no strings attached, are committed to the authority and the Lordship of Jesus Christ. The Bible says that if we walk in the light as He is the light, we have fellowship one with another, and the blood of Jesus Christ, God's Son, cleanses us from all sin. That's what it means to be of one heart and one soul.

It is the kind of commitment to each other where we respond to each other as brothers, in total honesty with each other, and where we can square off with each other, level with each other, be frank with each other, without either one of us accusing the other of having the wrong motives or of being bigoted or racist, the kind of eyeball-to-eyeball fellowship where we are willing to lay down our lives for each other. And I am convinced that if the social and political revolution, in terms of the black and white situation in America, continues to mount, Christians may well be called upon to give their lives for each other; there will be times when white brothers committed to Jesus Christ will have to stand between white reactionaries in their community and their black brothers in Jesus Christ, and there will be situations where black brothers committed to Jesus Christ will have to stand between black radicals in their neighborhoods and their white brothers in Jesus Christ. Because that's what it means to be brothers. And the black and white Christians in this country might as well face it now: the bond between people who are born of the Spirit of God of such a nature that all of us are in the same boat. They've got to face the fact that when white reactionaries and black radicals begin to fight it out with each other, you and I become their common enemy—even though we might be of the same color and from the same neighborhood. Because the issue is a spiritual one, and both the self-styled "revolutionary" and his opposite number, the secular "counterrevolutionary," are a great way from the Kingdom.

That is why we must be committed to a Christ Who belongs neither to the left nor to the right. That is the reason we've got to be committed to a Christ Who is neither black nor white. That's the reason we've got to be committed to a Jesus Who is neither a Democrat nor a Republican, neither a Communist nor a capitalist. He's the Lord from heaven; He's the Lord God, Who rules over the nations and over the affairs and destiny of men, and Who lives His life in those people who dare to trust Him. This is the kind of relationship that must develop through a commitment to Him. The kind of relationship that, if my white brother attends my church service on Sunday and some of my black brothers squawk, I must let my black brothers hear from me that morning, not next week. The kind of relationship where a white person who is committed to Jesus Christ will be willing to have his home burned down in the name of justice for his black brother and for the right of his black brother to buy a home in any community he wishes to live. The kind of oneness where we can raise our kids in the same church and, if they decide to get married to each other, let them live in peace. The kind of oneness where we raise our kids to trust God and to obey Him and to be available to Him, accepting the fact that God doesn't make mistakes. That's what it means to be intoxicated with God; that's what it means to be available to Him.

Verse 33 says, "And with great power the apostles gave their testimony to the resurrection of the Lord Jesus, and great grace was upon them all." Notice that they were intoxicated with Jesus Christ for the purpose of giving witness, giving testimony, telling the truth about the resurrection of Jesus Christ, the most important event in history. And as square as it may sound, and as evangelical and as fundamental as it may sound, that still remains the whole mission of the Kingdom of God: To bear witness to the resurrection of Jesus Christ. That remains the mission of the church, that is the essence of the gospel, that is the fundamental result of the gospel. It reproduces itself, and with boldness it tells men that Jesus Christ is alive, the "second man" has come to establish a new order and a new kingdom; here is a way out of frustration, there is a door open to man, there is a place where there can be true community, there is a place to stand where man can possess true and divine power.

Verses 34 and 35 say, "There was not a needy person among them, for as many as were possessors of lands or houses sold them, and brought the proceeds of what was sold and laid it at the apostles' feet; and distribution was made to each as any had need." There is no way anybody can deny that the gospel of Jesus Christ does not have social implications. Because people were available to Jesus Christ, their goods were available to Him, their money was available to Him. So that in the early church, in that fellowship of believers, no one lacked anything. These people were so available to each other that the hungry were fed, the naked were clothed, everything was done. They had none of the governmental programs we have today, yet no person was left destitute.

This is what James meant when he asked, What is pure religion? His answer: Pure religion is the feeding of the poor, the widows and the orphans, the taking care of the motherless and the fatherless. The man who is intoxicated with the life of Jesus Christ says, There are black people in this country who do not have decent food to eat because of racism, and I must do something about it. There are thousands and thousands of black people who because of racism are living in substandard housing, and I must become involved. There are black people who cannot dream of becoming President of the United States because of racism, and I must right this wrong. The person who is intoxicated with the life of Jesus Christ says, I must become involved in the burdens of people who are being held back because of sin and inequality and injustice. I must go out and put skin on God, I must make Him work, I must flesh Him out in my everyday life.

This must not only be true for the black and white relationship but also for the black and black relationship. The failure of being of one heart and one soul has also contributed to our holding ourselves back. The envy and the jealousy and the house-dividedness among us has also allowed the racism in our society to become so heavily entrenched. It is because the black man who has succeeded does not know how to bend down and lift his brothers up, and it is because those who were down did not help push the guy who was going up, that we've been held back. It has been the lack of love and respect, it has been the brainwashing by society, teaching us to hate ourselves, it has been the "house nigger" and "field slave" concept that has destroyed meaningful relationships among our own people—keeping in mind that when the ambulance goes screeching through the black community on Friday and Saturday nights, it is not going to pick up "Charlie," it is going to pick up what one black man has done to another. When in some black communities we consume twice as much liquor as anything else, depriving our children of milk and bread and ourselves of the economic power to build structures in our community, adding to the profits of the white man in the name of frustration, it is because we are not of one heart, we are not together.

The only One Who can put a man together, Who can put a community together, is Jesus Christ, Who makes men of one heart and of one soul. He sets men free, to be what God intended men to be. Those are the results of the gospel.

A man who is intoxicated with God, who has allowed the gospel to become a reality in his own life, reflects the life of Jesus. He lives oblivious to public opinion. He is in love, in a relationship that is thicker than blood brother or sister, with those other people who are intoxicated with God. He spends much time praising God. From one moment to another, he allows himself to be shaken from complacency and racism and hate and division and animosity. He speaks the Word of God with boldness and confidence. He is of one heart and one soul with every other believer. Those are the results of the gospel—a gospel which is genuinely black, even as it is genuinely white: multicolored, universal, the only hope for a sinful world in desperate need of God's redeeming grace.

Suggestions for Further Reading

Baldwin, James, *The Fire Next Time*, Dell Publishing Co., Inc.

Bennett, Lerone, Jr., *Before the Mayflower*, Penguin Books, Inc.

Brink, William, and Louis Harris, *Black and White*, Simon and Schuster, Inc.

Brown, Claude, *Manchild in the Promised Land*, a Signet Book, New American Library.

Buswell, James O. 3rd, *Slavery, Segregation and Scripture*, William B. Eerdmans Publishing Co.

Carmichael, Stokely, and Charles V. Hamilton, *Black Power*, a Vintage Book, Random House, Inc.

Cleaver, Eldridge, *Soul on Ice*, McGraw-Hill, Inc.

Conot, Robert E., *Rivers of Blood, Years of Darkness*, Bantam Books, Inc.

Grier, William H., and Price M. Cobbs, *Black Rage*, Bantam Books, Inc.

Hough, Joseph C., Jr., *Black Power and White Protestants*, Oxford University Press.

Jones, Howard O., *Shall We Overcome?* Fleming H. Revell Co.

Lomax, Louis E., *The Negro Revolt*, a Signet Book, New American Library.

Malcolm X and A. Haley, *The Autobiography of Malcolm X*, Dell Publishing Co., Inc.

Pannell, William E., *My Friend, the Enemy*, Word Books.

Report of the National Advisory Commission on Civil Disorders, Bantam Books, Inc.

Shriver, Donald W., Jr., *The Unsilent South*, John Knox Press.

Silberman, Charles E., *Crisis in Black and White*, a Vintage Book, Random House, Inc.

Skinner, Tom, *Black and Free*, Zondervan Publishing House.

Smith, Lillian E., *Killers of the Dream*, an Anchor Book, Doubleday and Co., Inc.

Stampp, Kenneth M., *The Peculiar Institution*, a Vintage Book, Random House, Inc.

Tucker, Sterling, *Beyond the Burning*, Association Press.

Warren, Robert Penn, *Who Speaks for the Negro?* a Vintage Book, Random House, Inc.

Wright, Nathan, Jr., *Black Power and Urban Unrest*, Hawthorn Books, Inc.

————, *Let's Work Together*, Hawthorn Books, Inc.

————, *Ready to Riot,* Holt, Rinehart and Winston, Inc.

Wright, Richard, *Black Boy,* Harper & Row.